Offshore Tax Planning Guides

Russell T. Potter

All rights reserved. Copyright © 2023 Russell T. Potter

COPYRIGHT © 2023 Russell T. Potter

All rights reserved.

No part of this book must be reproduced, stored in a retrieval system, or shared by any means, electronic, mechanical, photocopying, recording, or otherwise, without written permission from the publisher.

Every precaution has been taken in the preparation of this book; still the publisher and author assume no responsibility for errors or omissions. Nor do they assume any liability for damages resulting from the use of the information contained herein.

Legal Notice:

This book is copyright protected and is only meant for your individual use. You are not allowed to amend, distribute, sell, use, quote or paraphrase any of its part without the written consent of the author or publisher.

Introduction

This is a comprehensive resource that provides information and guidance on the tax implications and strategies associated with living, working, and investing offshore. It is designed to help individuals navigate the complex world of offshore tax planning and make informed decisions to optimize their tax situations.

The guide begins by discussing the benefits and considerations of living internationally. It explores the potential challenges individuals may face when leaving their home country, such as tax residency rules, reporting requirements, and expatriation procedures. It also highlights specific tax breaks available for living offshore, including incentives for moving to Puerto Rico.

For those working offshore, the guide covers important topics such as social security issues, expatriation, and strategies used by multinational corporations to minimize their tax liabilities, such as the Double Irish Dutch Sandwich and the "Check the Box" loophole.

The guide also delves into offshore business reporting requirements for individuals who operate businesses internationally. It provides insights into setting up foreign corporations, choosing the right jurisdiction for your business, and understanding the reporting obligations associated with offshore business operations.

Retiring internationally is another area covered in the guide, including the steps to take before retiring abroad, receiving social security benefits while living abroad, and the considerations of offshore pension plans.

Investing abroad is discussed, with an overview of the basics of international investing and the tax implications involved. The guide also addresses common myths and mistakes related to foreign trusts and explores the potential benefits of offshore foundations.

In the final section, the guide provides a roadmap for designing an international tax strategy. It outlines the steps individuals can take to optimize their tax situation, including considerations for residency, structuring offshore entities, and working with professionals experienced in international tax planning.

Overall, this book serves as a valuable resource for individuals seeking to understand the tax implications and opportunities associated with living, working, and investing offshore. It provides insights, strategies, and real-life examples to help individuals make informed decisions and develop a comprehensive international tax strategy.

Contents

Section One: Live Internationally 1
   Introduction to Section One 2
   Chapter 1: Leaving Might Be Harder Than You Think 5
   Chapter 2: Resident Reporting Requirements 8
   Chapter 3: New Tax Break for Moving to Puerto Rico 13
   Chapter 4: Special Tax Break for Living Offshore 17
   Chapter 5: Social Security Issues If You Work in Foreign Country 23
   Chapter 6: Taking the Big Step: Expatriation 26

Section Two: Work Offshore 32
   Introduction to Section Two 33
   Chapter 7: Do What the Big Boys Do in the U.S. 35
   Chapter 8: Double Irish Dutch Sandwich 40
   Chapter 9: The "Check the Box" Loophole 46
   Chapter 10: Quick C's: Customer, Capital, Cash 53
   Chapter 11: Three Real-Life Tax Offshore Stories 63
   Chapter 12: Where Will Your Foreign Corporation Live? 67
   Chapter 13: Offshore Business Reporting Requirements 70

Section Three: Retire Internationally 80
   Intro to Section Three 81
   Chapter 14: Five Things to Do Before You Retire Internationally 87
   Chapter 15: Receiving Social Security Benefits While Living Abroad 91
   Chapter 16: Pension Conversion When You're Offshore 94
   Chapter 17: Should You Have an Offshore Pension Plan? 97

Section Four: Invest Abroad 100

Introduction to Section Four 101
Chapter 18: Basics of International Investing.. 103
Chapter 19: Foreign Trust Myths and Mistakes... 106
Chapter 20: Should You Have an Offshore Foundation? 111
Section Five: Next Steps 114
Chapter 21: 5 Steps to Designing Your International Tax Strategy 115

Section One: Live Internationally

Introduction to Section One

Have you dreamed of moving to another country? Maybe you're fed up with the American lifestyle or concerned about where the U.S. is heading politically or economically. Or maybe you want to learn a new language or live more cheaply. There are a lot of reasons for wanting to live in another country.

I've lived in another country twice and my husband has lived in three different countries besides the United States.

My first stay outside the U.S. was for an unusual reason. We adopted our son David from an orphanage in Cd. Juarez, Mexico. In order to facilitate the process, I moved to the orphanage to live for 6 months. I moved there with a very specific purpose, and because I spent most of the time behind the four walls of the orphanage, I really didn't experience much of the country.

The second time that I lived in Mexico was with my husband, Richard, at the end of the real estate and stock market decline at the end of 2008. Nothing was happening with our businesses and so we moved to our beach house in Baja California. It seemed easier to just coast by the beach than try to fight a stagnated business market. By 2013, business was back and we moved back to the U.S. During that time in Mexico, we learned to speak Spanish, learned a whole new way of cooking and changed our living habits to a simpler and more environmentally gentle way of living.

For us, the possibilities of places to live doesn't stop at the border. Life is an adventure and with businesses like ours that are completely virtual, we can live anywhere.

Why do you want to move to another country?

The global bank HSBC recently asked international Americans why they wanted to move abroad. Here are their answers:

#1 Reason to Move: More Money! Most people surveyed wanted to advance their career or make more money and moving to another country helped with that. Interestingly enough, almost 2/3 of the people that moved abroad to make more money also decreased their expenses. And, for a whopping 87% of all surveyed who lived offshore when the recession hit, they never felt the effect of it.

<u>#2 Reason to Move: Expand Horizons!</u> The second most popular reason to make an international move is to see more of the world. More young adults have extended travel plans than ever before. Cheaper travel and the Internet have made more things possible. Sometimes the long trips extend into a permanent foreign address.

<u>#3 Reason to Move: It's Cheaper!</u> This is a big plus for retirees especially. Costs that go up as you get older, such as medical care, go way up in the U.S. There can be a point where the only way you can live in the U.S. is to really reduce your standard of living. If you move to another country, you can often have an even better lifestyle than in the U.S.

<u>#4 Reason to Move: Sick and Tired!</u> Almost a quarter of Americans living abroad are there because they got tired of their old home country. They cited immigration issues, tax, public spending, economic meltdown, crashing real estate market and social breakdown.

<u>#5 Reason to Move: My Honey is Going!</u> The 5th most common reason given for moving was that a significant other/spouse was moving to another country.

Whatever your reason is to think about moving outside the U.S., there are a few things to think about first.

That's what we're going to be talking about in this section. You'll learn about the impact living in another country might have on your U.S. tax situation, how to take advantage of a massive tax break and how simple it might actually be to qualify for it and the reporting requirements you can't afford to miss.

Even if all you're planning now is just to move out of the U.S., you'll probably also want to read the other sections dealing with retirement outside the U.S., investing offshore and working offshore.

Chapter 1: Leaving Might Be Harder Than You Think

There could be a lot of reasons for you to be thinking of moving out of the U.S. It could be for adventure, more money or simply for a change. If part of your plan is to reduce U.S. taxes, then you've come to the right place. There are some things you need to consider.

Where Are You Going?

If your plan is to save on taxes, it's important to think about the country you will move to. Some countries have higher tax rates than the U.S. does. This is important to consider if you're also planning on working in the country or plan to move your business there. Don't assume moving always means less tax, especially if you haven't first consulted with an experienced tax pro.

If your income will be all passive income, such as capital gains, interest or dividends, you could get a great new tax break in Puerto Rico. On the other hand, if you plan to work and have earned income, you can get a different kind of tax break provided you meet the requirements for foreign earned income deduction or credit as explained in Chapter 3: Special Tax Breaks for Living Offshore. And in some countries, you could have a problem with Social Security. Check out Chapter 4: Social Security Issues If You Work in a Foreign Country for the countries to watch.

You also need to make sure your new domicile will have banking available for Americans. Since FATCA (Foreign Account Tax Compliance Act) came into play on July 1, 2014, we have seen foreign banks banning Americans from setting up accounts. Some countries are a little easier for Americans to work in. Check this out first.

Be Careful How You Leave

Somewhere between deciding which country or territory you are moving to and actually packing up the storage container, there is some planning you need to do. One of those things to do before you leave is to make sure you're leaving from the right state.

If your last U.S. residence was in California, South Carolina, New Mexico or Virginia, you will find they continue to chase you for state income tax long after you've left.

The secret is to first establish residence in a different state, preferably a no-tax state.

Those non-tax states are Alaska, Florida, Nevada, New Hampshire, South Dakota, Tennessee, Texas and Wyoming. The most common states to move offshore from are Nevada and Florida.

Changing your state of residence will involve some steps. Let's say you move from a high tax state, such as California, to Nevada for a short period. And then, from Nevada you move offshore. If this all happened quickly, and without real evidence that the move to Nevada was a legitimate one, California might call foul. That means they will continue to come after you for tax in future years.

The problem is that the claim of state residency is subjective. There is no proven step-by-step guide to make sure a state doesn't chase you. There are some things that you can do to make a better case to avoid your previous state's tax.

- Purchase or lease a residence in a new tax-free state,
- Move household items to the new home,
- File a homestead exemption in new state,
- Register your children for school with your new address,
- Get a driver's license in new state,
- Register cars in new state,
- Open new bank account & safe deposit box in new state,
- Change address on credit cards,

- Register to vote in new state,
- File your federal tax return with the new address,
- Refer to the new address on all legal and trust documents
- Create a religious affiliation in your new state, if applicable
- Enroll children in sports, dance classes, etc. in new state,
- Change passport address to new state, and
- Join other organizations in your new state.
- Change your address with the Social Security Administration.

Make sure you can prove you really did set-up a new residence. The point is to be able to prove it wasn't just a sham to pay less tax.

Chapter 1 Review:

1. What steps do you need to take now to prepare for a future move?
2. Do you have past tax issues to clean up and, if so, what steps are you going to take now?
3. Make sure you use your new address every chance you get.

Chapter 2: Resident Reporting Requirements

It would be easy for me to lapse into the accountant-eze language in this chapter. I promise I'm not going to inundate you with tax code and dry rules and regulations. In this chapter, we're going to cover some basics of tax reporting. These are the unique forms that are required if you currently live offshore (or are considering it) or have an offshore business (or are considering it.)

If you miss filing these required tax forms, you could be looking at $10,000 - $250,000 or more in penalties and even up to 6 months jail time. And, these penalties may be assessed even if you owe no tax.

The IRS means business. They aren't just messing around. But, the good thing is that the reporting is pretty straightforward. This chapter is about the basics. This has become even more important as FATCA (Foreign Account Tax Compliance Act) was put into force on July 1, 2014. FATCA puts some teeth into the law plus requires foreign financial institutes to report on Americans with foreign bank accounts.

In the first place, you'll likely need to report on Schedule B of your regular annual Form 1040 Individual Income Tax Return. There is a box on this schedule that you need to check if you own, are a beneficiary of or are a signatory on a foreign financial account.

The next type of report is FinCen 114. The name for this form has recently changed; it used to be called TD 90.22-1. In 2014, the way you file it changed as well. The FinCen 114 is required if you had $10,000 or more in a foreign bank account at any time during the year. This return is due by 6/30 of the following year and must be filed electronically. There is no extension of time. There is no tax due with this tax form, but if you fail to file on time you can face penalties of $10,000 or even more. The FinCen 114 is due for individuals, partnerships, corporations and the like. If you have a foreign financial account, make sure you're in compliance.

The next form to consider is Form 8938. You need to file this form if you have a foreign account with more than either of the threshold amounts for your circumstances and/or meet certain other criteria, as shown below. You'll note that there are two different tables depending on whether you live in the U.S. or live outside the U.S. Under each chart, there are two rows. One is for single or married, filing separately. The second is for married, filing jointly. In each row under each table, there are two numbers. You will see "more than" and "end of year." If the total of your accounts was more than the number in the "more than" at any time during the year or if the total of your accounts at year-end is more than is shown in the "end of year', you will have to file Form 8938 with your regular income tax form.

For example, if you live in the U.S., you would use Table 1. Let's say you are single. If total of your foreign accounts was more than $75,000 at any time during the year, or you had more than $50,000 at the end of the year, you need to file this form.

Table 1:

Live in the U.S.	More than	End of Year
Single	$75,000	$50,000
Married, filing jointly	$150,000	$100,000

Table 2:

Live Outside the U.S.	More than	End of Year
Single	$300,000	$400,000
Married, filing jointly	$600,000	$400,000

Form 3520 is due when you have a transaction with a foreign trust, receive a payment from a foreign trust or have ownership of a foreign trust. You also need to use Form 3520 to report payments over a certain amount from an individual or from a corporation. This form is due at the same time as your individual income tax return, but you need to file the return separately.

If you transfer assets to a foreign corporation over $100,000 or if you own 10% or more of the company, you'll also need to file Form 926.

And then there are Forms 5471 and 8858, which are used for foreign businesses. We'll cover more information about those in Section 2: Work Offshore.

What Does FATCA Mean To You?

Besides piling on penalties if you miss reporting, FATCA also lays out some stringent reporting requirements for foreign financial institutions. It wasn't so long ago that there was the feeling that certain places like Switzerland or offshore havens in the Caribbean were sacrosanct. You never had to worry about the U.S. finding out about deposits or investments you had there. FATCA changes everything. Nothing is secret anymore. Let's take a step back and look at what FATCA actually is.

FATCA (Foreign Account Tax Compliance Act) came about in 2010 as part of the Hiring Incentives to Restore Employment (HIRE) Act. HIRE added chapter 4 to Subtitle A of the Code. "Chapter 4" is the term to remember here.

There are also a couple of definitions you will need to understand first.

Withholding Agent: A withholding agent or intermediary is an individual, corporation, partnership, trust, association or any other entity, including any foreign intermediary, foreign partnership, or U.S. branch of certain foreign banks, and insurance companies

U.S. Person: A U.S. person includes a U.S. citizen (even if they have another passport), U.S. resident alien, a domestic partnership, a domestic corporation, a U.S. estate, or a U.S. trust.

FFI: An FFI (Foreign Financial Institute) is any foreign entity that accepts deposits in the ordinary course of banking, holds financial assets for others (and this is a substantial part of its business) or is engaged primarily in the business of investing, reinvesting or trading in securities, commodities or partnership interests.

Participating and Non-participating FFI: An FFI that enters into an FFI Agreement to report information to the U.S. about U.S. depositors is called a participating foreign financial institute (PFFI). One that does not is a non-participating FFI. (NPFFI)

FFI Agreement: An FFI Agreement is an agreement between the IRS and the PFFI where the PFFI agrees to obtain info on account holders that is necessary to determine if accounts are U.S. accounts, comply with any required due diligence/verification, and annually report information on U.S. accounts. They also agree to deduct and withhold 30% U.S. tax on pass-thru payments to account holders that do not provide identification information or to a NPFFI.

The PFFI agrees to report the following information regarding U.S. accounts:

1. The name, address and U.S. tax identification number of each account,
2. In the case of any account holder that is a U.S. entity with one or more U.S. owners, the name, address, and TIN of each substantial U.S. owner of such entity,
3. The account number,
4. The year-end account balance or value, and
5. Gross receipts and gross withdrawals or payments from the account.

In essence, FACTA said that starting July 1, 2014, withholding agents have to withhold 30% tax on payments to foreign financial institutions (FFI) unless the FFI becomes a participating FFI. As a result, foreign tax planning for U.S. taxpayers had to come out into the light. And, as is the case, with a big and important change like this, there is a lot of misunderstanding and concern about the impact.

If you're late on any filings, get current right away. There are some amnesty programs available now that may help to reduce the penalties. Get with an experienced CPA right away to get current. Failure to do this can mean massive cash penalties and even jail time.

Chapter 2 Review:

1. Review the reporting requirements. Do you have a knowledgeable CPA that you're in good communication with regarding your foreign assets and filing requirements?
2. Do you have past missed filings? If so, what is your plan to get current?

Chapter 3: New Tax Break for Moving to Puerto Rico

Puerto Rico has turned into a recent hot spot for Americans considering a move offshore. Because it's so new, I want to highlight the benefits. Like any other tax strategy, it may or may not work for you.

New Puerto Rico Tax Break

Puerto Rico is a territory of the U.S. and as such still has a foot in the U.S. system. In some ways, it feels more familiar than other offshore locations. The new tax breaks are huge, if you plan right.

These new reforms are contained in Act 20 and Act 22. Act 20 helps businesses that locate in Puerto Rico. And Act 22 provides exceptional advantages for United States and Puerto Rican income tax filers. With proper planning, a U.S. citizen can reduce their U.S. tax to 4% on active income and completely eliminate most or all passive income tax.

There are generally four areas where you might benefit from a move to Puerto Rico. Do you have:

1. Capital gains? A move to Puerto Rico would completely eliminate the new huge rates for high net worth/net income individuals. These U.S. rates are now: federal marginal income tax of 43.4% on short-term capital gains and 23.8% on long-term capital gains. The tax may be zero with a move to Puerto Rico.

2. A plan for a service company that can be run from Puerto Rico (PR)? You can set up a Puerto Rican corporation or LLC and since you live in PR and do the work from there, income will not be subject to federal tax. The dividends or distribution that would be paid from the company to you are exempt from Puerto Rican tax. The tax on the company's profit would be just

4%. There is a tax of 33% on salary that you take from the company.
3. Ability to perform a function of your existing U.S. company in PR? If so, you could qualify for the same tax breaks as in (2) above.
4. A U.S. estate tax issue? This one is more specific to non-resident aliens. Non-resident aliens who invest $500,000 in Puerto Rico may receive a permanent residence visa. The benefit is that there will be no estate tax when the owner passes for assets that are located in Puerto Rico. U.S. estate tax will still apply for non-residents that have U.S.-based assets.

In order to qualify for these tax breaks you cannot have had residency in Puerto Rico at any time in the past 15 years and must have residency before 2035. There are two other requirements:

1. Bona fide Resident. The law defines a bona fide resident as someone that a) is present at least 183 days during the taxable year in Puerto Rico, b) does not have a tax home outside of Puerto Rico during the taxable year, and c) does not have a closer connection to the United States or a foreign country than to Puerto Rico. You can still be a U.S. citizen and be considered a bona fide resident of Puerto Rico. But, you need to be able to prove that you are closer to a resident of Puerto Rico than anywhere else.
2. Puerto Rican Sourced Income. Once it is clear that an individual meets the bona fide resident of Puerto Rico test, in order to be exempt from U.S. Federal Income Tax, he or she must also show that the source of that income is derived from Puerto Rico. Generally, the rules are similar to the rules for determining whether income is income from sources within the United States.

3. The law further notes that any income treated as income from sources within the United States or as effectively connected with the conduct of a trade or business within the United States shall not be treated as income from Puerto Rico. There are specific source of income rules that apply to each of the various forms of passive investments. Again, the Internal Revenue Code and Federal Regulations should be consulted for a complete understanding in order to effectuate the taxpayer's intended results. More information regarding taxation of interest and dividend income and capital gains follow.

1. **Interest and Dividend Income:** IRC Sections 862(a)(1) and (2) discuss when interest and dividends will be treated as income from sources within the United States. Generally, interest from the United States or the District of Columbia, and interest on bonds, notes, or other interest bearing obligations of non-corporate residents or domestic corporations (corporations organized in the United States or under the laws of the United States or any State) shall be treated as income form sources within the United States. In regard to dividends, amounts received as such from a domestic corporation and certain foreign corporations engaged in business in the United States will generally be treated as income from sources within the United States. Therefore, interest and dividends received from Puerto Rico residents and corporations organized under the laws of Puerto Rico will be Puerto Rico source income. However, this is so only to the extent of and subject to the applicability of the Conduit Rule and the 10% Shareholder Rule.

2. **Capital Gains:** Generally, capital gains from the sale, exchange, or other disposition of securities by a bona-fide resident of Puerto Rico are from sources within Puerto Rico. However, gains from the sale of securities owned by the

individual prior to becoming a bona-fide resident of Puerto Rico ("Pre-Residency Securities") will either constitute income from sources outside of Puerto Rico (unless a certain 10 year rule is met), or the portion of the gain attributable to the period prior to bona-fide Puerto Rico residency will be from sources outside of Puerto Rico, and the portion attributable to the period after bona-fide residency will be from sources within Puerto Rico.

As with any international tax strategy, work with a qualified advisor and make sure you're up to date on the latest tax law changes both in the U.S. and at your destination.

Chapter 3 Review:

1. Do you have passive income from investments that could be moved to Puerto Rico?
2. Would you consider moving to Puerto Rico in order to get a huge tax break?
3. Do you have an experience CPA on your team with ties to Puerto Rico, or who is familiar with the law?

Chapter 4: Special Tax Break for Living Offshore

In the Foreward to the book, I talked a little bit about our history in other countries. During our last time in Mexico, I started an outsourced bookkeeping service. Because it was clearly foreign income earned in Mexico, Richard and I qualified for the foreign earned income tax credit/deduction at the time. Here's how it works.

Foreign Income

This income must be earned in the foreign country. You could get a job and make the foreign income by working for someone else. For most of my clients, though, they make money with their own business. This could be something like the outsourcing firm we set up. Or, like I often see with my clients, it could mean arranging an online business so that it's clearly income earned outside the U.S.

The second part of this is to remember it is earned income. In Chapter 3, we discussed Puerto Rico, which has some new tax laws that reduce tax on passive income. That's only for Puerto Rico though. For all other countries, you're going to be looking for the Foreign Earned Income Deduction or Exclusion, if you qualify. That means earned income. It's not applicable for interest income, dividend income or capital gains.

Foreign Earned Income Exclusion Amount

If you qualify for the deduction, by having foreign earned income and a foreign residence, you can take an exclusion of up to $99,200 (in 2014). That's $99,200 per person. So, a married couple that both qualify would have an exclusion of almost $200,000. The IRS adjusts the possible exclusion amount each year.

Foreign Housing Allowance

In addition to the foreign earned income exclusion, you can also claim exclusion for housing. Just like the foreign earned income exclusion, your tax home has to be in a foreign country and you qualify for the exclusions and deduction under either the bona fide residence test or the physical presence test.

The housing exclusion applies only to amounts considered paid for with employer-provided funds. That includes any amounts paid to you or paid or incurred on your behalf by your employer that are taxable foreign earned income to you for the year (without regard to the foreign earned income exclusion). The housing deduction also applies to amounts paid for with self-employment earnings.

Your housing amount is the total of your housing expenses for the year minus the base housing amount. The base housing amount is calculated as 16% of the maximum foreign earned income exclusion.

Housing expenses do not include expenses that are lavish or extravagant, are incurred buying property, purchasing furniture or accessories, or improvements and other expenses that increase the value or appreciably prolong the life of your property.

If you excluded meals and lodging from your business income or deducted meals and lodging as part of your moving expenses, you can't also get credit in the exclusion for that amount.

Additionally, foreign housing expenses may not exceed your total foreign earned income for the taxable year. Your foreign housing deduction cannot be more than your foreign earned income less the total of your (1) foreign earned income exclusion, plus. (2) your housing exclusion.

Both the foreign earned income exclusion and the foreign housing are calculated and reported on Form 2555 – Foreign Earned Income.

Physical Presence and Bona Fide Residence Test

In order to take advantage of the foreign earned income exclusion and foreign housing exclusion, you must have:

1. Foreign earned income, and
2. A qualifying foreign residence.

There are two different ways to prove you have a qualifying foreign residence. The two tests are the bona fide residence test and the physical presence test. You don't need to pass each test, just one.

Bona Fide Residence Test

Of the two tests, the bona fide residence test is a little more subjective. You have to prove that you have a residence in another country. That's pretty much it, but you do have to meet some additional rules.

Minimum Time in Residence

As part of the Bona Fide Residence test, the federal government and the IRS have established a minimum time in residence when living in a foreign country. In order to pass this test you must have lived in the foreign country uninterrupted for a minimum of one full tax year. This means a period that includes twelve full months. Bear in mind that the tax year begins on the 1st of January and ends on the 31st of December. If you were to move into a foreign country on any day of the year other than on the 1st of January, you will have to wait until the following year to claim this exemption. If you leave the country before the end of the year, you also cannot use the bona fide resident test to qualify for the foreign earned income test.

Visits Home Do Not Affect Your Filing Status

As stated just above, you need to have a foreign residence for the entire tax year. But, that doesn't mean you can't ever go home. While you are required to spend an entire tax year in the foreign country in order to claim this exemption, there are a few exceptions to this rule. You are permitted to leave the country for business or vacation purposes without affecting your filing status. These trips must be relatively short in duration and it must be quite obvious that you intend to return to your home in the country you happen to be residing in.

Permission to Live in Foreign Country

If you wish to meet the requirements set by this policy, you must become a resident of the foreign country you are living in. In most instances, you will need a visa in order to stay for an extended time in a country. When you file for that visa, you will state whether you do or do not wish to become a legal resident of the country in question. And then, of course, the government of your host country must agree with your plans to be able to live and work in the country.

You are not considered a bona fide resident of a foreign country if you make a statement to the authorities of that country that you are not a resident of that country. Also, if the foreign country authorities hold that you are not subject to their income tax laws as a resident, you're not a resident. If you have made such a statement and the authorities have not made a final decision on your status, you are not considered to be a bona fide resident of that foreign country. To be considered a bona fide resident of a foreign country, you have to pay tax in the foreign country.

Bona Fide Test Doesn't Always Work

It is important to note that just because you live in a foreign country for an entire tax year, it does not mean that you automatically meet the bona fide residence test.

Example:

If you go to China to work on a particular joint venture project for a specified period of time, you will be temporarily in the country. Ordinarily, you will not be regarded as a bona fide resident of that country. That is true even though you might work there for one tax year or longer. The length of your stay and the nature of your job are only two of the factors to be considered in determining whether you meet the bona fide residence test. In this case, you haven't demonstrated your intent to make this your home.

The bona fide residence test applies to U.S. citizens and to any U.S. resident alien who is a citizen or national of a country with which the United States has an income tax treaty in effect. Thus, you must determine if a treaty exists if you are a resident alien.

Tax Due to the Country Where You Claim Bona Fide Residence

It's also important to note that if you claim to be a non-resident of the foreign country to the foreign country's government and therefore do not pay income taxes to such government, you would not be able to qualify for the foreign earned income exclusion under the bona fide residence test.

The bona fide residence test, like the physical presence test, comprises one way that an individual can qualify for the foreign earned income exclusion. You may still qualify under the physical presence test if you do not qualify for the bona fide residence test.

IRS's Bona Fide Residence Determination

The IRS answers questions of bona fide residence on a case-by-case basis. They will take into account such factors as your intention or the purpose of your trip and the nature and length of your stay abroad. You must show the IRS that you have been a bona fide resident of a foreign country or countries for an uninterrupted period that includes an entire tax year, January 1st to December 31st. The IRS decides whether you qualify as a bona fide resident of a foreign country largely on the basis of facts you report on Form 2555, Foreign Earned Income. The form must be filed before the IRS will make a determination.

The Physical Presence Test

The physical presence test is a different test than the bona fide residence test and as such there is a different approach. In order to meet the physical presence test, you must have been physically present in the country for a minimum of 330 days. These 330 days must have all been within a continuous twelve months. The definition of a full day is a time period of 24 hours. The IRS does not count travel days in that count.

Of the two, the physical presence test is the more certain. It's just a matter of counting the days and being able to prove where you were and when. The bona fide residence test provides more flexibility, but it's more complicated and there is less certainty that the IRS will agree. You can also run into problems with some countries that required months, or even years, to receive residency.

Chapter 4 Review:

1. Do you plan to qualify for the foreign earned income exclusion and the foreign housing exclusion?
2. If so, will your income clearly be foreign and earned?
3. If yes to (1) and (2), which test are you planning to Use to establish residency?
4. How will you document the residency test?

Chapter 5: Social Security Issues If You Work in Foreign Country

If you move to another country, you may want to go to work there at some point. We've covered some tax tips such as foreign earned income exclusion and foreign housing exclusion, what states to leave the U.S. from (as last residence) and new IRS reporting requirements so far in this section. In this chapter, we're going to talk about Social Security, not collecting it, but paying it.

The problem is that if you go to work for a company in another country, you could end up paying in for both Social Security (to the U.S.) and a Social Security-equivalent in another country.

To avoid this problem, the U.S. has bilateral Social Security agreements with 25 countries. This is how it works.

Bilateral Social Security Agreements

The U.S. began entering bilateral Social Security agreement over 40 years ago. These agreements coordinate the U.S. Social Security program with the comparable programs of other countries.

Bilateral Social Security agreements are also called tantalization agreements or international social security agreements. These agreements have two purposes:

1. They eliminate dual Social Security taxation,
2. They fill in gaps in benefits if you have divided their careers between the United States and another country.

The aim of all U.S. bilateral agreements is to eliminate dual Social Security coverage and dual Social Security taxation and still give the best possible coverage for the workers.

It's not up to you to decide which system you like best. That's all been laid out in the agreements. The agreements all do not change the basic coverage provisions of the participating countries' Social Security laws. They will simply exempt you from coverage under the system of one country or the other when work would otherwise be covered under both systems.

These agreements clarify how to handle two Social Security systems while you work, but they have the added benefit of providing benefits when a worker has retired or become disabled and otherwise not received benefits.

If you would like more information about the United States' Social Security bilateral agreements program, please write to:

SOCIAL SECURITY ADMINISTRATION

Office of International Programs, P.O. Box 17741

Baltimore, Maryland 21235-7741

Existing Bilateral Agreements

Following are the 25 countries with agreements, the date of the agreement and a link for more information for that country and its agreement.

> Italy In force: 11/1/78
>
> Germany In force: 12/1/79
>
> Switzerland In force: 11/1/80
>
> Belgium In force: 7/1/84
>
> Norway In force: 7/1/87
>
> Canada In force: 8/1/84
>
> United Kingdom In force: 1/1/85
>
> Sweden In force: 1/1/87
>
> Spain In force: 4/1/88
>
> France In force: 4/1/88
>
> Portugal In force: 8/1/89
>
> Netherlands In force: 11/1/90
>
> Austria In force: 11/1/91

Finland In force: 11/1/91

Ireland In force: 9/1/93

Luxembourg In force: 11/1/93

Greece In force: 9/1/94

South Korea In force: 4/1/01

Chile In force: 12/1/01

Australia In force: 10/1/02

Japan In force: 10/1/05

Denmark In force: 10/1/08

Czech Republic In force: 1/1/09

Poland In force: 1/1/09

Slovak Republic In force: 5/1/14

If you are planning to work in a country that doesn't currently have a bilateral Social Security agreement, you can write to the Social Security Administration and ask them to negotiate one. There's no guarantee that they will, of course, but they are actively soliciting suggestions.

Chapter 5 Review:

1. Do you plan to work in a foreign country?
2. If yes, does your foreign country have a bilateral Social Security agreement? If not, how will this impact your net income, after taxes?

Chapter 6: Taking the Big Step: Expatriation

US. citizens living in other countries are often called "expats", but this does not mean that they have gone through the formal process of expatriation. Expatriation is the process you go through that ultimately means you no longer are a U.S. citizen. It's a big step, but, for some people, it is a vital one both for economic and non-economic reasons. In this chapter, we're going to look at what it actually means to expatriate, whether it's something you should consider and probably most importantly, what expatriating is not.

Why Do People Expatriate?

There are two main reasons why people want to leave the U.S. system permanently: concern about where they see the U.S. heading and the feeling that it's getting too expensive to stay in the U.S.

When someone expatriates, there is a cost to the U.S. The U.S. gives up the right to tax revenue and loses productive people and businesses from the country. It means jobs and wealth move outside the U.S.

There can also be a cost to the person expatriating. We'll talk more about that in this chapter.

How to Expatriate

In order to expatriate, you'll have to do some paperwork. You'll have to have an exit interview at an Embassy or consulate and you'll then receive a Certificate of Loss of Nationality, assuming all goes well. The interview is to make sure that you understand the gravity of what you're doing, that you're not crazy and that no one is forcing you against your will. Usually the process is pretty matter-of-fact.

The Year You Expatriate

Your tax return in the first year you expatriate will be a little different. You will have 3 tax returns to prepare:

1. Form 1040. This is your normal Form 1040 Individual Income tax return and you will report income from January 1st up until the date when you terminated your citizenship.

2. Form 1040NR. Use this form for your income from the day following your exit interview up until December 31st. Normally this return just shows income that comes from U.S. sources. Remember since you're no longer a U.S. citizen, you no longer have the responsibility to pay tax on worldwide income.

3. Form 8854. This is the tough one. You may have additional tax due because of your expatriation. To get to the answer, there are some calculations you'll need to do. If you are a covered expatriate, you're going to pay some additional tax.

Calculating Your Exit Tax

Are you subject to the exit tax? Well, let's look at the first, broad-brush test. Did you have an average income tax liability of more than $157,000 for the past five years? Or, is your net worth $2,000,000 or more? If so, you need to take a look at this.

The calculation for income tax liability is also adjusted by certain credits, so even if you seem to need to hit the limit, you actually may not.

But let's say that you do qualify. Now what?

In June 2008, a bill was passed to provide benefits to returning veterans. This was the Heroes Earnings Assistance and Relief Tax Act (HEART Act). This same Act also created a new tax Section 877A that became effective for U.S. taxpayers who want to leave the U.S. tax system and give up their citizenship. Under the new expatriation tax law, effective for years beginning in 2009, "covered expatriates", i.e. those who have a net worth of $2 million, or 5 year average income tax liability exceeding $139,000 (adjusted each year for inflation), are treated as if they had liquidated all of their assets. Once the net gain, difference between the asset's fair market value and the taxpayer's basis, is calculated, any gain greater than $680,000 per taxpayer will be taxed as income in that calendar year.

If you didn't sell the asset, it doesn't matter. This tax applies whether or not you have an actual sale.

This tax law also applies to deferred compensation plans, pension plans, stock options and the like. The current fair market value of these will be taxed as well, even though you may not have cashed them out.

One of the common strategies to reduce or eliminate this exit tax is to gift away part of the assets to reduce the amount of assets.

Does Expatriation Make Sense?

Putting aside the emotional issues on either side of the decision (to stay or to go), there are some good arguments that have an effect on both sides.

The IRS has a test to determined whether you are a covered expatriate or an uncovered one. If you're covered, you'll pay taxes when you expatriate. The back of the envelope test to see if you might be covered is:

- Your average annual net income tax for the 5 years ended before expatriation date is more than $157,000 for 2014. (This amount adjusts annually.),
- Your net worth is $2 million or more, or
- You fail to certify you've complied with all U.S. federal tax obligations for the past 5 years.

The actual test is more complicated than this, but it should give you an idea if you should be concerned about being covered.

Here are 7 problems with expatriation that many people miss:

1. Extra taxes. If you're a covered expatriate you may be taxed on assets that are illiquid, unvested compensation and assets that you don't even completely own yet. You may get caught with

both U.S. and foreign government taxation on the exit tax. Gifts made by expatriates may be subject to more tax once you have expatriated.

2. Past Compliance Issues. If you've had a tax compliance issue in the past, no matter how small, you may become a covered expatriate and have a lot more taxes.

3. Covered Expatriation Test is Complicated. You may have high income and not be subject to the exit tax. There are some credits to apply. If you're covered, you may have a lot of tax. If you're not covered, you have no tax. The difference between the two could be a complicated formula. The simple

4. Estate Planning Will Get Even More Complicated and Expensive. The lifetime and estate tax exclusion will not be available. The rules on trusts and gifts get very confusing.

5. Personal Residence Exclusion Lost. If you have a personal residence, sell it before you go through the expatriation process. Otherwise, the gain will be taxable without the $250,000 (single) or $500,000 (married, filing jointly) exclusion.

6. Double Taxation. When you expatriate, you pay an exit tax on your assets, even if you haven't sold them. Then, when you do sell them, you may have to pay tax again in your new home country

7. Tax Due on U.S. Source Income. You may be surprised to learn you still have to file U.S. tax returns and pay tax after you leave. In fact, you'll be subject to mandatory 30% withholding on the gross amount of U.S. distributions unless you file the Form W-8 BEN, Form W-8 BEN-E. or Form W-8-ECI. Things often get more, not less, complicated after you exit the U.S.

That's the problems that you might not consider with expatriation, now let's look at the benefits.

Let's clear up a few myths you might have heard about expatriation.

1. Myth: Only a few people expatriate every year. Fact: The government doesn't count how many people actually do expatriate. They only count the covered expatriates. In other words, if you don't qualify as a covered expatriate and pay an exit tax, you wouldn't be counted in the number. One consulate along averages 3 applications per day, day in and day out. Obviously there are a lot more expatriations than the few thousand we hear about. It's almost like the government doesn't want you to know how many people really are making the move.

2. Myth: Everyone has to pay an exit tax when you leave. There is a tax, but only if you are a covered expatriate. There is a lot of bad tax information out there. For example, one wrong rumor floating around is that you have to pay a certain tax (somewhere between 10% - 20%) on all of your net assets when you leave, no matter what. That's simply not true.

3. Myth: You can only spend 30 days in the U.S. OR you just need to spend 181 days out of the U.S. Once you expatriate, you are not a U.S. citizen. The number of days per year you can spend in the U.S. will depend on the visa you get. Remember, you're no longer a U.S. citizen with the rights and responsibility of citizenship. However, if you spend more than 120 days (180 days under some tax treaties) in a year in the U.S., you will become subject to worldwide income.

4. Myth: If you expatriate, you can't come back to the U.S. In 1996, the Reed Amendment to the Immigration and Nationality Act was passed to allow the Attorney General the right to deny entry into the U.S. of anyone who renounced citizenship to avoid taxes, has a communicable disease, has been convicted of crimes involving moral turpitude or illegal drugs or is a prostitute, spy, terrorist or draft evader. Most of that isn't going to be applicable to you. Even though it's been almost 20 years

since the new Amendment was enacted, there are still no regulations.
   5. Myth: You're going to lose Social Security benefits. This is simply not true. In most cases, there are no restrictions on non-citizens receiving benefits they have earned with a couple of exceptions. If you move to Cuba, North Korea or Iran, you can't get the benefits, though. That's because there are currently trade restrictions for those countries. You could find that your Social Security benefits will have a mandatory 30% withholding.

Is expatriation for you? Perhaps. There are many things to plan for, especially if you're going to end up being a covered expatriate. You can plan with gifts and trusts to reduce or eliminate the impact of the exit tax. Get good advisors who are experienced with this and put the plan in place first.

Chapter 6 Review:
   1. If you are considering expatriation, is there a chance you will be considered a covered expatriate?
   2. If so, is there a strategy to reduce that? That could include making gifts, setting up a trust or becoming compliant on past tax issues, if that is the problem.
   3. Have you reviewed the items to consider that may be problems you hadn't anticipated?
   4. Have you put together your legal and tax team to help you with the transition?

Section Two: Work Offshore

Introduction to Section Two

The fastest growing segment of my tax practice is people who want to move themselves and/or their business out of the U.S. In the last section, we talked about some of the tax and reporting strategies for moving yourself outside the U.S. We also talked about taking the big step of expatriation.

In this section, we're going to talk about moving your business offshore. That could mean that you move as well. In fact, if you do, it's a lot easier to prove a non-U.S. tax situation. But, even if you continue to live in the U.S., you can still own a business that is U.S. tax-free or almost tax-free.

It goes without saying that moving a business offshore is controversial. There is a lot of concern that the globalization of businesses leaves U.S. citizens without jobs and a diminished life style. But, for that matter, there are some who criticize me for telling people how to pay less tax, with the idea that everyone else should pay more tax so the person criticizing gets more benefits.

In this section, I'm not going to address those issues. I'll assume that if you're interested in learning the tax rules and strategies to move all or part of your business offshore that you've already dealt with concerns about moving business and possibly jobs offshore. If this is a problem for you, please skip this section.

In the following chapters, we'll cover:

- How the big companies do it, and how their tax-saving strategies could work for you,
- Basics of building a legal offshore tax system, and
- Real-life stories of clients where it worked and some where it didn't.

If you also move to a foreign country, you'll want to check out the foreign earned income allowance and foreign housing allowance.

We covered that in Chapter 4: Special Tax Breaks for Living Offshore.

In Section 2: Work Offshore, we're going to look just at the business and some benefits from moving all or part of it offshore.

How can you use offshore tax laws to your benefit? Here are some tips:

If you live in the United States, you will pay U.S. tax on the income you earn. If you use a foreign corporation, you won't be able to work in it while in the U.S. and avoid U.S. taxes.

If you retire to a foreign country and your only income is from a pension, Social Security, U.S. based investments or real estate, you will continue to pay U.S. income tax.

If you live abroad, work for a U.S. company, foreign employer or your own business that is located abroad, and if meet the foreign earned income exclusion requirements, you'll be able to exclude $99,200 in income from your U.S. income tax return for 2014. And, if married and your spouse has the same circumstances, the amount will double. The exclusion amount adjusts annually.

If you run a foreign business, live and work abroad, meet the foreign earned income exclusion requirements, and operate through an offshore corporation, you may be able to eliminate all U.S. tax on your ordinary income.

Chapter 7: Do What the Big Boys Do in the U.S.

French economist Gabriel Zelman recently concluded a study about society and taxes in general. Some of his findings:

- The actual corporate tax rate paid by U.S. corporations has dropped from 30% to 15% since the late 1980s, even though the tax rates have not changed, and
- 20% of all corporate profits in the United States have been moved offshore.

You don't need to reinvent the wheel when it comes to creating an offshore tax strategy. There are plenty of examples of what big companies are doing and how it saves them tax. Of course, they also often have large staffs of CPAs and lawyers, making sure they are following the strict letter of the law through some pretty complicated transactions.

In this chapter, we're going to look at some of the most notable companies and the tax-saving strategies they use. We're also going to look at some simpler versions of the same strategies. Could some of these strategies work for you?

How Apple Does It

Apple Inc. made news in 2013 when the U.S. Senate called on them to look at the strategies they used to dramatically reduce the taxes they paid. They avoided paying $12.5 billion in U.S. taxes on the income earned on 2011 and 2012. There was a lot of bad publicity for Apple, although they were very forthcoming about the strategies and the amount of taxes they had saved. Despite some negative reports, the fact is that everything they did was legal. Laws may change in the future, but every time a new law comes into play, there are people like me who find new legal ways to pay less tax.

Apple has had a tax-reducing mindset from the beginning. The less you pay in tax, the more you have to grow your business and, the more you have available to pay employees in salary and benefits. And, of course, the manager, inventors and investors are rewarded as well.

Apple doesn't have just one tax strategy with a magic "get out of tax jail free" card. They have multiple strategies that have been thoroughly researched, properly implemented and of course, reported with full compliance with applicable government regulation. It's not a strategy of being sneaky or illegal. It's simply taking advantage of what is available. The main offices for Apple are in Cupertino, California. But they have business structures in other states and countries.

First, let's look at the domestic tax-saving strategies that Apple has used.

Nevada Offices

Apple set up a Nevada subsidiary in 2006 called Braeburn Capital. (Braeburn is a type of apple.) This company handles investments for Apple. The operations are in Nevada, and so the income will stay in Nevada, a tax-free state. In this way, they are creating Nevada income, but using assets that were originally in California. California has some of the highest state tax rates and Nevada has no state income tax. It's a pretty smart move.

One possible challenge is a new California state law that states that California income tax is due if 25% or more of your clients are located in California. So, Braeburn needs to find a way around that if it handles only Apple Inc.'s assets.

Apple has gotten a lot of the press about offshore tax strategies, but there are other big companies using similar strategies. For example, Google, Amazon and Hewlett-Packard have moved offices to Nevada. They aren't necessarily moving cash and investments over to Nevada offices like Apple, but instead they are moving royalties. Here's how it works.

Companies like Apple, Google, Amazon, Hewlett-Packard and Microsoft make money not just by selling a physical product but also from selling the uniqueness of it. That all has to do with the intellectual property that has been established by brand trademarks and patents.

The brand identifies the company. For example, I have used Apple products for years. I identify my computer as a MacAir. I have an iPhone. I have an iPad. There is a powerful brand at work there!

But there are also things that these products do that have to do with the programming and physical attributes of the devices. These are covered by patents.

There is a value to that intellectual property and that value can be established separately from the product itself. So, you might pay $500 for an iPod, but you're buying more than just a pretty screen and case. You're buying the programming that makes it all work. That programming is covered by a patent, so there is another asset that you've bought. For every iPad sold, a portion of that profit goes to pay for the use of the intellectual property (IP). The IP is an intangible asset and doesn't really exist in the physical world. That means the ownership can be separate from the company creating and/or selling the physical product. The company has now created an income stream that can be held separately in a tax-free state.

I used Apple products as an example above, but the same thing is true for Microsoft products, Amazon products and the like. My Kindle has IP as well, and that IP can be held in another company, in another state.

The actual steps in order to make this work are:

1. Establish IP through the use of trademarks, servicemarks and patents,

2. Own the IP in another state (usually Nevada),
3. Establish a fair price for use of the IP by the main company, and
4. Pay, on a regular basis, for the use of the IP. (This moves income from the company's home state to a tax free state.)

Other times, the products themselves are digital. For example, downloaded songs or educational webinars are digital. It is much easier for a businesses and digital products to move profits to low-tax states or even low-tax countries. A downloaded application can be sold from anywhere.

Will This Work For You?

There was a time when Nevada corporations were very popular. It was thought that all you needed to do was just set up a Nevada corporation and then you'd never pay tax in your home state again. That wasn't true, and the states, particularly California, have been vigorously seeking out people who improperly use a Nevada corporation to make their money in their home state and then not pay state income tax on that income.

The problem is that there has to be nexus associated with the income you earn. Nexus means connection. If you have a connection with a state, you will have to collect and pay sales tax and/or pay state income tax in that state. If you set up a company in another state, you need to make sure you also have nexus in that state. Just saying you have a Nevada corporation, for example, doesn't mean you have Nevada income.

You earn money in a state because you fulfill services there, install products there, have offices there, have employees there or even promote through trade shows or seminars there. Any of these activities you could create state nexus. And that, of course, means you have some state income tax and/or state sales tax to pay.

However, if you can legitimately set up a business, have an office and have work performed in another state, you may be able to move income from a tax-heavy state to a tax-free state.

Before you jump into an offshore tax strategy, make sure you are first taking advantage of all U.S. tax strategies available to you.

Chapter 7 Review:

1. Do you have a strategy to save taxes on business income within the U.S.? It's easier and cheaper to develop U.S. tax strategies.

2. Have you set up IP for your business? If not, do you have a plan to do so? Who will own the IP?

3. Do you have good accounting and contracts between your companies to back-up any business income and expense between your companies?

Chapter 8: Double Irish Dutch Sandwich

We can't talk about Apple and other big companies and their offshore tax strategies without talking about some pretty interesting strategies like Irish, Double Irish and Dutch Sandwiches. In this chapter, we're going to go through the process that some of the large corporations use to maximize the use of favorable tax laws in other countries.

Please note that these are legal at the time of the writing of this book. However, there is a lot of talk about closing some of these international tax loopholes. It's possible that by the time you're reading this chapter, that we've had a lot of changes in this arena. To keep up, please make sure you're registered at http://www.TheOffshoreTaxGuide.com for the latest in tax planning. You'll also receive free coaching for a month when you register your book.

We're now going to look at some of the terms you might have heard in the news.

Double Irish

A Double Irish strategy requires two Irish companies. This is often used for intellectual property that is held outside the U.S. One of these Irish-formed companies is then tax resident in a tax haven country such as the Cayman Islands, Bermuda, or any of the other dozen or so tax haven countries.

Irish tax law allows for an Irish company that is tax resident in another country to not be subject to Irish tax. That is provided that the central management and control is not located where it is incorporated. In other words, an Irish company that is tax resident in Bermuda and with management outside Ireland, will not be subject to Irish tax. This offshore Irish company owns the U.S. IP rights.

The IP rights are then licensed to a second Irish company that is tax resident in Ireland. There are high royalties and fees paid to this company. This company receives income from use of the IP rights in countries outside the U.S. But it has to pay fees then to the first Irish company that is tax resident in a tax haven country. In other words, the U.S. company pays a high licensing fee to the second Irish company, who in turns pays licensing fees to the first Irish company that is tax resident outside Ireland.

The end result is a deduction for the U.S. company that is never taxed anywhere else as income.

The Double Irish strategy is used by Abbott Laboratories, Adobe Systems, Eli Lilly and Company, Facebook, Forest Laboratories, General Electric, Google, IBM, Johnson & Johnson, Microsoft, Oracle Corp., Pfizer Inc., Starbucks and Yahoo, among others.

Dutch Sandwich

Apple also uses a strategy called a Dutch sandwich. This is added to the Double Irish to further reduce tax liabilities. Ireland does not levy withholding tax on certain European Union member countries. The Netherlands is one of those countries.

Here's how it works: Move your money to Ireland, then the Netherlands, and finally to a tax haven such as Bermuda, but following a very specific plan.

1. Develop intellectual property (IP) in the U.S.

2. Set up a corporate subsidiary in Ireland, and sell (or license) foreign rights to the intellectual property from (1) above. This Irish company will be tax resident in a tax haven country. Please note that this law is changing, after pressure from the U.S. Effective January 2015, under current law, Ireland will no longer allow Irish companies to be tax resident in tax haven countries. They must all be tax resident within Ireland starting in 2015.

3. Foreign profits based on intellectual property go to the tax haven resident Irish company. The U.S. parent company pays

U.S. taxes only on the fees that the Irish subsidiary pays back to the U.S.

4. The Irish tax haven resident company will need to purchase the IP rights that were developed in the U.S. To make this strategy work as efficiently as possible, have the subsidiary pay as little as possible for use of the licensed intellectual property. This shifts the maximum amount of profit to Ireland and away from the U.S.

5. Now, set up a second Irish corporation. Your first Irish company will own this company. The second company will do the work of selling products and recording revenue. This second company is Irish tax resident.

6. The profits from the second Irish corporation (Irish tax resident) is run through a third subsidiary corporation in the Netherlands. Ireland has tax-free transfers inside some countries in the European Union. The Netherlands is in one of them. The profits from the second Irish corporation are now in Holland.

7. Now, route that profit from the Netherlands company back to the first Irish subsidiary, which is tax haven resident.

The Irish companies are the "bread" and the Netherlands company is the "cheese". Hence, this strategy is referred to as the Dutch sandwich. "

There are also Luxembourg and Swiss sandwiches. The middle part of the sandwich just needs to be a European Union country that Ireland does not assess a tax on for transfer.

How Other Companies Do a Double Irish

Like Apple, Google is located in California. Google shifts profits into an Irish subsidiary that is tax resident in Bermuda and so there is no Irish or U.S. corporate income tax on that income.

Google has been questioned by the U.K. Parliament twice over its tax affairs and is in a more than $1 billion dispute with French tax authorities. Yahoo! Inc. additionally has a Dutch sandwich tax strategy. They have funneled hundreds of millions of dollars in profits through a Dutch bookkeeper's suburban home office en route to subsidiaries in Mauritius and Switzerland.

Yahoo is also a California-based company that has deposited profits in an Irish subsidiary that claims not to be a tax resident in Ireland, but instead in the Cayman Islands.

It will be interesting to see what happens with strategies after 2015, when Irish laws change to no longer allow tax haven residency for Irish companies.

Forest Laboratories, based in New York, has used virtually identical strategy to that of Google, claiming most of its profits are offshore, even as its sales are almost entirely in the U.S. The difference between Google and Forest Laboratories' strategies and that of Apple is that Apple is claiming income from foreign sales and IP is offshore. Forest Laboratories and Google seem to be running all sales through foreign companies. If that is the truly the case, Forest Laboratories and Google are taking a more risky approach.

But it's not just Ireland and Netherlands that provide tax savings. Cisco Systems Inc. is based in San Jose, California. They attribute about half of their worldwide income to a tiny town at the foot of the Swiss Alps.

Will This Work For You?

I occasionally get inquiries from prospective clients about 'doing something like Apple did. Can you do a double Irish Dutch sandwich? Sure, as long as you do it before January 2015. After that, the strategy will change.

The thing is that while you may be able to set up the same structure, you may not be able to take advantage of it. There are a couple of common denominators in the cases we just discussed. First, they had something they were selling and making money at. This strategy isn't for moving passive income or selling a service that was clearly associated with the U.S. The product was sold globally. Apple moved only the offshore sales (current at the time of the report) through the offshore strategy. Other companies have taken some U.S. sales through offshore companies. I think that's a little more difficult to prove.

If you have a digital product that you are selling, it would probably work more easily with an offshore plan. You may sell the IP rights to an offshore company. You then create a way to upstream some or all of the profit to the offshore company. You may also fulfill the product offshore. If you had developed the product in the U.S., there would still be some U.S. tax due. On the other hand, if the product was developed offshore, you may be able to escape completely tax-free. This actually could adapt to an easy strategy without having to add two Irish companies, a tax haven link and a European Union company that is friendly with the Irish tax structure.

You may also have a product or service that has IP associated. If you also have overseas sales, you probably could set up something to save on U.S. taxes.

For most small business owners, the complex strategies that Apple, Google and other big businesses use don't make sense. You may save a lot in taxes but you'll pay even more in fees to setup and maintain the companies and to keep current with the tax law changes. However, in the right circumstances, you may very well be able to save a lot of taxes and do it in much simpler way. In the following chapters in this section, we're going to go over the basics of setting up an offshore business and share some real-life stories from our clients.

First, though, we're going to look at one more strategy that the big boys use. We'll cover that in the next chapter.

Chapter 8 Review:
1. The offshore tax strategies discussed in this chapter were fairly complicated. Do you have a business with foreign sales and IP

that could take advantage of these strategies?
2. How much savings would you need to see to justify the time and expense required to set up and run the strategies?
3. Do you currently have a CPA and an attorney on board who have the experience to help you with such plans?

Chapter 9: The "Check the Box" Loophole

There is one more offshore tax strategy used by big companies. It's known as "Check the Box."

The 'Check the Box' Strategy

There has been a lot of press about the so-called "Check the Box Loophole." I've read the most popular articles on the Internet. Most were wrong. So, please just disregard anything you might have heard before about this specific tax strategy. Let's start fresh.

The 'check the box' term comes from the taxation of LLCs (limited liability companies). This particular strategy started when there was a tax question regarding how LLCs (limited liability companies) would be taxed. It isn't very new. In fact, 'check the box' strategy started in 1995, during the Clinton Administration. This allowed LLCs to select how they wanted to be taxed. There is no such thing as an LLC tax return, so it was important for the IRS to determine how the LLCs would file.

There was another decision to be made. What happened if an LLC owner didn't make a choice on how to be taxed? That's when the IRS came up with the notion of default tax treatment. If there are two or more owners, the LLC defaults to a partnership return. If there is just one owner, then it is called a disregarded entity and it is simply merged with the tax return of the one owner.

The LLC, in the case of offshore companies, is the foreign wholly owned subsidiary of the domestic corporation. The LLC takes advantage of offshore tax breaks and then just merges the foreign LLC into the main company. There is no need to report transfer from one company to another. It's all part of the same company.

This is a crucial point with a part of the offshore strategy of the big boys. To demonstrate it, let's look at one more big business that takes advantage of the domestic and foreign tax laws to save a lot of taxes.

Microsoft's Plan

While Apple keeps most of his low-taxed foreign income offshore, Microsoft has been able to hold more of its reserves in the U.S. Their overall strategy may look similar to Apple, but there are a couple of differences. Here's how it works.

In a recent Senate investigation, they found that Microsoft reduced its 2011 tax bill by $2.43 billion by using a wide, international network of controlled foreign business.

Microsoft Corp. does 85% of its research and development in the U.S. Of its 94,000 employees, 36,000 are in product R & D. It also has a substantial workforce in Reno, Nevada, taking advantage of the state tax-free climate. That business is Microsoft Licensing, GP which licenses out Microsoft's IP for joint ventures with outside companies.

Their overall strategy uses foreign companies set up in Ireland, Puerto Rico and Singapore. These tax haven resident companies hold intellectual property rights.

Microsoft has 3 main revenue sources from its intellectual property. The first is from retail software when it is sold to consumers, retailers and enterprise licenses to governments and businesses. The second is for web products such as Microsoft Bing and Xbox Live. And, the third, is licensing to computer manufacturers who pre-install Microsoft software on products they sell.

In the 1990s, Microsoft established three regional centers, one in Ireland, one in Puerto Rico and one in Singapore. These offices handle retail sales. The Ireland office oversees all retail operations in Europe, the Middle East, and Africa. Singapore oversees all operations in Asia. Puerto Rico oversees all operations in North, Central and South America.

These three sales locations, plus Microsoft Corp (U.S.), pay a portion of profits for Research & Development (R & D). The Ireland office pays 30% of profits, Puerto Rico pays 25%, Singapore pays

10% and Microsoft U.S. pays 35%. Microsoft U.S. also handles bulk sales to computer manufacturers.

In exchange, Microsoft Ireland, Microsoft Singapore and Microsoft Puerto Rico get the right to sell the retail products in their corner of the world and Microsoft U.S. gets the right to sell licenses to manufacturers. Here's a little more in-depth discussion of what's going on.

Microsoft Operations Puerto Rico (MOPR) holds the right to sell in North, Central and South America. MOPR makes digital and physical copies of Microsoft software to sell in its designed territory.

So, for example, when I go to my local Office Depot in Reno, Nevada to buy a copy of Microsoft Office, I'm picking up a copy that was produced in and shipped from Puerto Rico.

Hang on, because this is where it gets more confusing. MOPR, a Puerto Rican company, produced and distributed that product you bought in the U.S. MOPR is actually owned by MACS Holdings. This is a Bermuda-based entity. MACS Holdings is owned by an Irish company, Round Island One, which is tax resident in Bermuda. Round Island One is owned by Microsoft Corp (U.S.).

Since the trail all comes back to Microsoft Corp, you might wonder why that copy of Microsoft Office wasn't sold directly by the main company. The reason is taxes. Over 3 years, Microsoft saved $4.5 billion in taxes on goods sold in the U.S. alone.

Microsoft Ireland Research (MIR) holds the right to sell Microsoft products in Europe, the Middle East and Africa.

Unlike the plan for sales in the Americas with MOPR, MIR doesn't actually create or sell any products to any customers. Instead, MIR licenses the Microsoft intellectual property rights to **Microsoft Ireland Operations Limited (MIOL)**, a wholly owned Irish subsidiary.

MIR and MIOL are fully owned by **Round Island One**, the Irish company that is tax resident in the Bermuda. You might remember Round Island One from the previous American tax strategy.

MIOL manufactures copies of Microsoft products and sells them to distributors in the territory. Microsoft did not pay any U.S. tax on any revenues made by the Irish groups.

No U.S. tax was paid on the $9 billion license payment from MIOL to MIR.

Microsoft Asia Island Limited (MAIL) holds the right to sell in Asia. However, MAIL is actually located in Bermuda and has no employees.

MAIL pays a portion of profits to Microsoft Corporation for retail sales in Asia. MAIL licenses its rights directly to **Microsoft Operations Pte. Ltd (MOPL)**. Again, no taxes are paid on this amount. MOPL duplicates the Microsoft software and sells them to distribution entities around Asia.

MAIL and MOPL are both wholly owned subsidiaries of **Microsoft Singapore Holdings Pte. Ltd.** This company is then a disregarded entity foreign subsidiary of Microsoft Corp.

How Check the Box Works

The operations shown above for Microsoft avoid all or most U.S. taxes by moving operations and companies to tax haven countries. At this point, you can probably see how similar the Microsoft strategies are to Apple and others we have discussed.

However, there is one big difference with Microsoft's overall plan. Other big corporations with foreign branches may have used this strategy to some extent and by the time this book is published, it may have even great use.

This additional strategy has to do with the "check the box" regulations that allow these foreign subsidiaries to collapse back into the parent company. Although they are taxed separately, the wholly owned foreign-taxed subsidiaries of Microsoft Corp are all LLCs that have taken disregarded entity status. That means the financial statements collapse into the giant Microsoft Corp. They are taxed differently, but for all intents and purposes, they are financially joined.

The financial statements for the company show all the profit from all the subsidiaries. So, the shareholders see how much money the company is making for them. But, the U.S. tax returns do not show the subsidiaries. That is how the strategy of 'check the box' or, more accurately, the disregarded entity status works for LLCs.

When asked about the complex strategies that Microsoft Used to avoid U.S. tax, a representative from the company explained that the complex structure was a response to the complex tax code.

"Microsoft has a complex business and we must comply with the complicated tax code of the United States, resulting in an exceedingly complex tax structure."

One benefit of the disregarded entity status is that financial statement income will be increased by the foreign income. No tax due, but the financials look better. The other benefit, and perhaps the biggest one, is that the cash from the foreign companies is lumped in with the U.S.-taxed income. In Chapter 10, I'm going to talk about how bringing cash back from a foreign company is almost always taxed.

In this case, the disregarded entity status means that the cash is not subject to U.S. tax. This is the huge loophole that you might hear bandied about.

Will This Work For You?

In short, will a complex plan of multiple wholly owned foreign subsidiaries that handle overseas sales, research & development and/or intellectual property save you taxes? Perhaps. But, it might not be the best plan for you. It's expensive to set up and run, so you may be trading less tax for much higher professional fees. There is also an assumption that you have intellectual property and that there are overseas sales that can be fulfilled offshore. If you don't have those parts of the plan, it may not work at all.

Still, there are a few simplified strategies you may add after you've reviewed these complicated plans. If you have offshore sales, why bring the income back to the U.S.? If you have a plan to keep income offshore in investments such as precious metals and real estate, you may be able to defer U.S. tax. You also won't need to report these assets since precious metals and international real estate are exempt from reporting.

You may also sell intellectual properties rights to an offshore entity and then upstream income to an offshore entity to reduce U.S. taxable income. Or, you could set up a strategy to bring some of the cash back, understanding that you'll pay some U.S. tax on the cash when you repatriate it.

The Next Step

There are three things that all of the big companies we discussed have in common.

First, they plan far in advance. Apple set up their first Irish subsidiary company just four years after they were founded. Think back to the company then. They released Apple III as their first venture into the business market. It was before iPhones, iPods or Ipods. It was before Macbooks, MacAir or any of the dozen other products that have made Apple billions of dollars. To see the future that would come that early on took an amazing amount of foresight. Tax planning done in advance saves tax dollars. The further in advance you can do it, the more money you will save.

Secondly, they had a strategy and implemented it with the best professionals. They didn't go cheap and try to do-it-yourself, but instead hired experienced lawyers and CPAs to put the strategy in place.

Third, they maintained the strategy and updated it as necessary. This is where an ongoing relationship with attorneys and CPAs come into play. The CEO of Microsoft isn't reading tax law, or if he is, he's just doing it to make sure he's speaking the same language as his CPAs and attorneys.

The people who get in trouble with offshore tax strategies for their business and investments typically make mistakes by listening to the wrong people or trying to shortcut the system and assume that no one will find out. The IRS is on to the scams and focusing a lot of attention on people who try to go offshore with their income in the wrong way. In the next chapter, we're going to look at some of the basic strategies to set up an offshore business the right way.

Chapter 9 Review:

1. What is your overall plan with investments or business offshore?
2. What will you do with the money you make or save offshore?
3. Will you bring the money back into the U.S., and, if so, do you know how much U.S. tax it will cost when you do?

Chapter 10: Quick C's: Customer, Capital, Cash

Before we get into what you can do, I've got a strong warning for you. Sometimes it may appear that there is a fine line between offshore tax fraud and international tax planning. Offshore tax fraud is a crime. You can go to jail for it and be fined hundreds of thousands, maybe millions of dollars. On the other hand, international tax planning is legal. It is not generally simple or cheap to set up a legal international tax strategy and keep it current, but if you want to pay less tax, it can be a great way to save money. That is, provided you follow the rules and implement legal strategies.

The offshore tax industry is filled with scammers and promoters. If the offshore promoter isn't a U.S. attorney or a currently licensed CPA, he or she should not give you any U.S. tax advice.

The best way to avoid offshore tax fraud is to follow the advice of a U.S. tax expert. After all, if the point is to set up your entity in a tax haven jurisdiction, the only tax you need to be concerned with is U.S. tax. So you don't need an offshore tax expert, you need a U.S. tax expert. You do need someone to set up the offshore entity and to properly maintain it. You'll need someone to help you with the offshore bank account and you may need someone to help you set up your offshore offices or whatever you need to establish nexus in a foreign country.

Here are some examples of a few offshore tax fraud schemes that you should avoid:

Susan lives in New York and has been told that she can set up a foreign Charitable Foundation in Panama. She's also been told that any money that Susan contributes to the foreign foundation will be deductible on her U.S. tax return. It's not taxable in Panama, and so she's got tax-free money in Panama. Or, at least, that's what she has been told.

Right? Wrong. The only tax-deductible charitable contributions you can make are to U.S. charities. It is possible that a foreign charity has received U.S. non-profit status, but don't assume it's true.

You can make a deduction to a qualified 501 (c) (3), 501 (c) (9) or other qualified non-profit organizations. You can take a deduction for the contribution. But you don't get to just use the money any way you want. You can't operate a non-profit like your alter ego. The problem with this foreign charitable foundation scheme is that it won't create deductions unless the charity is also an authorized U.S. charity. And even if it is authorized as a U.S. charity, you won't be able to use the money for your own personal use.

The Right Way

If you don't have a charity in mind, you can set up a U.S. charity. If you want to create a family foundation, you can do the same thing in the U.S. or offshore. But, you won't get a tax deduction from U.S. taxes for contributions to the foundation if it's offshore and not authorized in the U.S.. In some cases, you can set up a family foundation that will allow you make contributions and can be used to fund some activities such as scholarships. This is sophisticated tax planning and definitely needs to be undertaken with an experienced tax professional.

We will discuss foreign foundations in more detail in Chapter 21. A foundation isn't necessarily taxed as a charity, so make sure you know what you're getting into before you get a foundation.

The Wrong Way

One IRS red flag to be concerned with is if you're told that that you must keep everything secret. You shouldn't be publishing details about your financial life on social media, but it can also be a warning if the entire strategy is built around hoping no one finds out. In fact, thanks to some new regulations, you'll have to make reports about your assets to the IRS or face huge fines and even jail time. Make no mistake, privacy is one of the benefits of offshore tax planning, but this doesn't mean you can get sneaky about your financial details with the IRS.

The Right Way

When I devise a plan for a client, I understand that it will be reported to the IRS, must be in tax compliance, and I assume that any major creditor will find out what steps we took and where the assets are located. If the assets remain private, that's great, but proper asset protection puts up barriers the creditor can't breach. It is not simply hiding assets at the risk of running afoul of the IRS.

Another version of the 'keep it a secret' strategy is a system that uses nominee directors. There can be a legitimate reason for having nominee directors, but don't think this is going to get you out of your U.S. tax obligation.

When the IRS looks at an offshore tax plan, they look at what the economic substance actually is. In other words, what is the purpose beyond just saving on taxes? Do the actions make sense?

Note that when the IRS analyzes a tax plan, they focus on the economic substance of the transaction. You can have someone stand in your place as a nominee director, but if it's your company, it's your company. You still control it. Having a nominee director doesn't make a single bit of difference in your tax plan.

You might have heard about 2% plans. They've been popular in both the U.S. and offshore promoter markets. This refers to a plan where you sell 98% of your U.S. business for a small sum to an offshore business. You retain just 2% of the company, hence the name '2% plans.' The theory is that if 98% of your company is owned by a foreign company, then 98% of the income can float off to a tax haven.

There are many things wrong about this plan. You didn't sell a big chunk of the business for a reasonable sum. The transaction doesn't have any economic substance. And, a domestic business is required to report ownership by a foreign owner. Plus, there is a mandatory

30% withholding on distributions from U.S. businesses to foreign entities or individual owners. There is a way around this by reporting the foreign ownership and having the foreign company agree to file and pay U.S. tax on the distributions. If you do that, though, you've defeated the whole plan to avoid U.S. tax. In short, this plan won't work.

If you have a problem with the set-up due to a lack of economic substance, you will probably find you've got a tax problem. In fact, if that was the purpose of the set-up, you probably are facing a charge of offshore tax fraud. However, it is possible to make transfers to offshore accounts in order to have another layer of asset protection. In that case, transactions like this could be very useful. Offshore asset protection usually does not increase or decrease your U.S. taxes. You do have to file additional returns with the plans, though, so there is a maintenance cost to them.

So, How Do You Build a Legal Offshore Tax Strategy?

We talked about some common offshore tax schemes that could mean your tax plan is really an illegal tax scam. And, in the previous chapter, we discussed some of the plans that the big companies use to legally reduce the amount of U.S. tax they pay.

Now, let's look at some simple, foundational rules for setting up a legal offshore tax strategy.

Easy C's

I call these the Easy C's. If you control and are aware of these three things right from the start, you're much more likely to have a strategy that will work.

The first C is customers (or clients). Where are your customers located? Where are they making the purchase? Where is the product or service being fulfilled? What assets do you Use to make that sale?

Here are some examples of what might work, and what might not.

Example #1:

You sell a new electronic gadget that is all the rage in the U.S. You notice that you are starting to get inquiries from Europe. Is there a way to make money from the sales to Europeans and not pay U.S. tax?

Answer: This case has the first part of the Easy C: Customer handled. You clearly have customers outside the U.S. However, if you're fulfilling from the U.S. – taking customer service orders, assembling and/or shipping – you've still got U.S. source income. Additionally, if the gadget is sold through just one website portal, you're going to have some complication separating out the U.S. customers from the foreign customers to determine which is U.S. income and which is foreign. In this case, all of the sales will look just like regular U.S. sales.

If you set up a foreign website, owned by an offshore company, so that people outside the U.S. could buy through another process, than you quite possibly have foreign source income. That would mean the income is probably not subject to U.S. tax because the sale is to foreign customers, the process is handled offshore and the ownership of the website is by a foreign company.

However, if you start commingling your U.S. sales and your foreign sales, you're not going to be able to achieve the separation you want to keep a foreign income stream U.S. tax free.

Example #2:

You have an Internet site with digital downloads. You have customers all around the world, but it seems like your product is really hot in Asia. Your whole business is in the U.S. because you're in the U.S. Is there a way to move some of the business outside the U.S. to legally avoid tax?

Answer: You clearly meet the prerequisite for customers outside the U.S., but you also need to look at fulfillment and the product itself.

Chances are your digital downloads were created in the U.S. That means you have U.S source income, unless you create separate digital downloads to be sold to your foreign markets. Your website was likewise created in the U.S. That includes articles, web copy, blogs, etc.

One strategy would be to move foreign customers to another website, with different content and digital downloads that were created offshore. The ownership of this website would be a foreign company.

Or, you could have the foreign company purchase the rights to the digital downloads. The value would need to be established by an independent appraiser. It would then require that some of the income would come back to the U.S. and that would be taxable.

Example #3:

You have a bricks and mortar business and you're adding a website to also sell the same products to your U.S.-based customers. You wonder if you can move the website business to a foreign company because you're invisible on the Internet anyway.

Answer: This one isn't going to work. The clients are from the U.S. and the income is U.S.-sourced.

Example #4:

Let's say you have a service business, something like preparing U.S. tax returns. Part of the tax preparation business is for U.S.-based citizens and some of the tax preparation business is for foreign nationals who have U.S. business or investments and need a U.S. tax return prepared. Can some of the business be considered foreign and thus not subject to U.S. tax?

Answer: Okay, I confess! The service business discussed here is my business, USTaxAid.com. We provide full tax services for small business owners and investors. We have a growing number of foreign nationals that are our clients. So, is there a way to turn this business stream of income into something that is tax free in the U.S.? After all, there are clients who do not live in the U.S.

In this case, the work performed is done in the U.S. So, it is U.S. based income.

However, if I moved out of the country, or some of my USTaxAid Services CPAs did, the income could be considered foreign income and there would likely be foreign income exclusions available, as discussed in Chapter 4.

C is for Cash

One of the big questions you need to answer when you start a foreign company is what are you going to do with the cash. Unfortunately, it's also one of the areas where the rules are often misunderstood. And there are some offshore promoters out there giving plenty of bad information. If you follow it, you're the one who will pay the price.

That's why the second C of the Easy Cs is "cash."

Although I've been talking about tax-free income in this book, the fact is the income is usually tax deferred, not tax free, for most U.S. citizens. You don't pay U.S. tax now if you set up your offshore business correctly. But if you bring the cash back to the U.S., you'll probably pay taxes.

Here are some possible business offshore strategies for dealing with the cash of what works and what does not work:

Thumbs Up!

A client came to us who had a business that could easily have a legitimate offshore business presence. They had foreign customers and could either sell the IP rights to the assets that generated the business to a foreign company or they could develop a similar product offshore and create foreign IP. In that way, they could pass the test of foreign customers and fulfillment. But, was that enough?

In this case, the client also said that they wanted to start buying real estate offshore. That means that they had a plan to invest the cash into assets outside the U.S. They had no plan to bring the money back to the U.S.

So far, so good. They could very well have a winning plan. But, of course, they need to make sure it is implemented correctly and that all of the required IRS reporting is done.

Thumbs Down!

A new client had run into an offshore promoter before he talked to us, and he either didn't understand exactly what the promoter was saying or the promoter miss-sold the way an offshore company worked. Once the sale was done, this promoter didn't have any interest in helping the client understand.

In this case, the client had been told that he could move money offshore and then trade the funds to make income. He could bring all of the money back to the U.S. without paying any tax. That was because he's done it through a Panama foundation.

You can't legally bring back income to the U.S. and not pay some kind of tax.

And, perhaps most importantly, you must report your holdings in an offshore account. If you don't report, you could face penalties of $10,000 - $250,000 and jail time of up to 6 months when you get caught.

There is one more option. You could follow Microsoft's plan and set up a foreign wholly owned subsidiary and do the 'check the box' regulations to collapse back into the U.S. company. Could you do it? Yes. But should you? Perhaps not. This would be an expensive structure to set up and maintain. Plus, you'd need to make sure you have products and services that would fit the model. And, what I think is the biggest concern, Congress may close this loophole any time now. There is a lot of talk about it and how it's not fair to the

U.S. to allow big corporations to do this. And, of course, if the big corporations can't do it, neither can the small corporations.

It's more expensive. It's more complicated. There is much more IRS scrutiny. And, it could be shut down any time now. For those reasons, I would not recommend it.

C is for Company

A foreign corporation that is owned and/or controlled by U.S. owner(s) is known as a controlled foreign corporation (CFC). We'll be using that designation (CFC) to describe the company that is owned by U.S. taxpayers.

A foreign corporation with U.S.-based owners often actually means tax deferral. At some point, the money is probably coming back to the U.S. The U.S. owners are subject to tax if the profits are paid out in the form of dividends or as liquidating dividends when the foreign corporation is sold.

That's part of what you need to consider if you set up a CFC. You may qualify to not pay taxes now, but what is your exit strategy? If you continue to live in the U.S., you'll probably have to pay taxes at some point because ultimately that money will come back to the U.S.

There is also additional cost to consider when you compare operating a business offshore versus running a business in the U.S. If you're not located physically where your business is, you may find you have a lot more costs in the form of employee and fulfillment mistakes, travel costs and just generally, a drop off in the business because you're not there to take care of it.

You need to also be careful regarding laws in the foreign country. For example, some tax haven countries do not allow international businesses to compete with local businesses. If you try to run a foreign business from the U.S., you'll most likely create a U.S. source for the income again. And that means you've got U.S tax due.

While you're physically in the U.S., you can't engage in any significant operational or management activities if you have a CFC.

If you're already working virtually or your business is completely virtual, it will be easier to run your company from another location. But the rules are still the same; you cannot be THE business. You'll need people outside the country to help you.

This is where we need to take a step back. Can you accomplish the same tax savings by making full use of U.S. tax strategies?

The bottom line is to not get too enamored with one plan. There are a lot of tools at your disposal. An offshore business could be right, but if it's too complicated you're going to pay a whole lot more in fees and costs for running the CFC in a foreign land. And after all this work and expense, you may find that all you're doing is deferring taxes to a time when tax rates have gone up.

The Easy C's are customers, cash and company ownership. If you address each of these factors with your offshore business, your plan will be a lot easier to implement and run.

Chapter 10 Review:

1. Do you have a business that might be able to legally set up an offshore company?
2. Where will your customers come from?
3. How will you fulfill on the sales with goods and services?
4. Would you consider moving outside the U.S. to qualify for both the foreign income exclusion and solidify the foreign tax treatment?
5. Do you have an exit strategy for your foreign businesses if you're planning to stay in the U.S.?

Chapter 11: Three Real-Life Tax Offshore Stories

We've talked about a lot of hypothetical situations and big company examples so far in the book. Let's look at some real-life examples of what has worked and what has not for our clients. Our clients are all small business owners or investors. Do any of their circumstances sound like your own?

Case #1: One Foot in Mexico

We'll call these clients Bob and Susan. They live part of the year in the high tax state of California and part of the year on the beach in Mexico. Bob was an author who traveled all over the U.S. speaking at paid events. Susan had an online digital download business that could basically be run from anywhere.

They wondered how they could take advantage of the foreign earned income exclusion.

That's when we had to sit down and talk about the rules. There are two:

1. You must have foreign earned income, and
2. You must pass the physical presence or bona fide residence test.

So first, we had to look at the type of income they had. Did it qualify as foreign earned income? The primary source of their income came from Bob's speaking engagements. He had to show up to be paid. And those gigs were all in the U.S. That meant the income was U.S. source. We could actually stop right there. Unless they had income that was created and sourced outside the U.S., this plan isn't going to work.

One possible solution would be to write the books outside the U.S. and then sell the books outside the U.S. This would create a foreign I.P. At least a part of the income could be tax-free or tax deferred.

The foreign income exclusion or deduction also requires that you have a physical presence or bona fide residence. For these taxpayers, they would clearly not qualify for the physical presence test. They are in the U.S. too much. So, their only chance would be to qualify for the bona fide residence test. They would need to have one residence and that is in the foreign country. They need to have a visa that allows them to work and live in the foreign country. Their visits to the U.S. need to be short. And, as we mentioned before, Bob needs to find a way to do work outside the U.S.

When we went through all of the details, we discovered that they probably could not qualify for the foreign income exclusion at this point.

Case #2: Here Come the Europeans!

An offshore attorney referred Ted to our company. Ted had the company set up correctly, but he wasn't quite sure how to use it. And that's why he came to us.

As we talked, we discovered that he had a web-based company. The service was fulfilled from the website and the sale was made at the website. He started the company assuming it would be primarily a U.S. company but soon found that it was a hit with Europeans. That's when he decided to form a company in a tax haven country. But, now what?

He had the customers from outside the U.S., but unfortunately his entire fulfillment was done through a website, which was developed in the U.S.

In order to make use of the foreign income that has been generated and legally avoid U.S. taxes, Ted has a couple of options:

1. Sell the U.S. IP to the foreign company, or
2. Create new foreign IP.

The website itself could be set up so that the IP address is detected and a U.S.-based customer goes to the U.S. site and everybody else goes somewhere else. Or, this could be set up so that the customer sees an opening page that shows a 'click here for the U.S.' and 'click here for non-U.S.'.

Once the foreign income is clearly separate from the U.S. income, Ted needs to make sure that the income from the sales is properly allocated as well. The U.S. income goes through a U.S. bank account for the domestic company. The foreign income goes through an offshore bank account for the tax haven-based company.

There will be a U.S. tax return to file for the domestic company and likely there will be some tax due from the foreign company (depending on how the I.P and website are handled.)

In the end, though, the strategy works. But, it wouldn't have worked without thoughtful implementation.

Case #3: Offshore Implementation

Angela lives in the U.S. She is not interested in changing residence, at least for now. She came to us after her business had been in place for a while, and now she was trying to figure out how to make sense out of the puzzle she had.

Angela started off providing a financial consulting program. At first, it was a more typical fee-based, one-on-one service. Over time, though, she developed a system that created an analysis based on questions. That analysis could be done through the computer. The computer program also calculated a list of things to do to implement the financial plan. Most of that required some human intervention. That work was done offshore as well.

Angela had been using a domestic company for the income and expenes, but now she wondered if there was a way to do this offshore and save on U.S. taxes.

There were two things that were true for what Angela was doing:

1. She had created the IP in the U.S. and she continued to manage the business from the U.S.

2. The clients were all from the U.S.

Until Angela got around these two obstacles there weren't a lot of other options, other than possibly creating a separate profit center for just providing the services.

This is one strategy that is going to take a couple of conversations to really nail down what Angela wants and what she's willing to change to make it easier to achieve that goal.

Chapter 11 Review:

1. Do you currently have a business that could have a foreign component?
2. What would you be willing to do to save on U.S. taxes? Would you move to another country? Would you set up another website? Would you create IP in another country?

Chapter 12: Where Will Your Foreign Corporation Live?

If you have an offshore tax strategy, at some point, you'll need to set up a foreign company. And that leads to the next question: Where?

The answer to this, and most tax questions, is "It depends." First, know your strategy. For example, if your income is going to be coming from China, a Hong Kong company is the best solution for you. You may have a business that will lend itself to a Double Irish Sandwich, like the big boys use. That is, assuming the laws still allow them.

Each offshore location and entity type has its own advantages and benefits. Generally speaking, most owners are looking for anonymity, good asset protection and a reduction in U.S. taxes.

If your business fits the requirements discussed in the previous chapter, than you may be able to move all or part of it out of the country. Assuming you want to move to one of the tax haven countries, you now have another choice. Which country is right for you?

Remember that your business is going to need to do business. It will possibly enter into contracts, open bank accounts and sell various goods and services. You probably will need to employ people through your international business. So, you need to pick a country that you can easily work in.

Four criteria to consider when you're choosing the right country:

1. Cost to incorporate and annual renewal fees,
2. Reputation,
3. Processing times and costs, and
4. Ease of banking.

The ongoing costs are important to consider, but if you're doing a real offshore set-up to save tens of thousands or more in taxes, it might not be as critical as making sure you can work easily in that country.

Reputation refers to that country's reputation in the business community. For example, Anguilla has long been a favorite among experts that set up offshore businesses. That reputation comes from having solid business laws and quality legislation that supports businesses. It also indicates a general confidence in the country's stability.

Processing times refers to the time to complete the formation of the offshore company including preparation of the corporate documents. Some countries can promptly register businesses while others have a lengthy and generally more costly process. This is a reflection on the effectiveness of the local government agencies and registered agents.

The final concern I've listed here is probably the most important right now. It's how the banking system works. In fact, since the July 1, 2014 impact of the Foreign Account Compliance Tax Act (FATCA), banking has become a real problem in some areas. FATCA requires foreign financial institutes to provide a long list of information on deposits for US citizens or businesses owned by them. It has become a big paperwork problem for these businesses and, to avoid it, some countries simply no longer allow deposits by Americans or their companies. And, that includes not allowing bank accounts of foreign companies that are owned by Americans. When FATCA came into law on 7/1/14, there was a very strong, and perhaps unreasonable response to it. Most likely as time goes on, the foreign financial institutes will ease up on their reaction and things will go along more smoothly.

As a CPA, my main concern will be making sure you are properly reporting in the U.S. It doesn't matter to those reports whether you form your entity in Anguilla, Panama, Belize or some other tax haven country.

Chapter 12 Review

1. What is your plan for a foreign business? Don't start with the entity; start with the plan.
2. Have you reviewed your plan for your business with a CPA with offshore business experience? What changes will you need to make to your business model?
3. Which country did you decide to set your business up in?
4. What type of entity will you use? The answer is determined by the foreign country's tax law and tax treaty with the U.S.
5. What is your exit plan from this company? (ie, how do you get the money out?)
6. What are your next steps after reviewing this chapter and questions?

Chapter 13: Offshore Business Reporting Requirements

This is the place where you can determine whether the offshore strategy you're being pitched is legal or not. If you're told that you never have to report anything, that no one is going to know and that you can sneak money back into the U.S. with no tax…RUN! It is not legal. And the penalties when you get caught are very stiff. You're looking at a minimum penalty of $10,000 and up to 6 months in jail.

But, I Didn't Know!

A few months ago, an investment advisor approached me about one of his clients. She was in a real tax jam. She was a recent widow and her husband had always taken care of their substantial holdings. She was also the sole beneficiary of a sizable trust in Canada.

She filed her tax return and didn't think twice about it, because she reported all of the income she received. But now, the IRS had showed up for an audit of one of her businesses and, in the process, discovered the Canadian trust.

She hadn't filed the returns she needed to report the foreign financial holdings. There was no under-reporting of tax, she just didn't report that she had the trust.

The penalty for that was 50% of the trust, or a little over $1.4 million. She didn't know, but that wasn't a defense. The IRS was being very tough.

There is a lesson here for all of us. File the right paperwork at the right time. Trying to cut corners can cost you big-time in penalties.

Required Information Tax Filings

First, you will need to make sure you're in compliance with the individual reporting requirements we discussed previously in Chapter 2: Resident Reporting Requirements.

The individual tax reporting requirements may include:
1. Indicate on Schedule B of your Form 1040 that you are a signator on a foreign financial account,
2. File FinCen 114 by June 30th, and/or
3. File Form 8938 with your Individual Form 1040.

You additionally need to include business foreign financial accounts on the Form FInCen114 if the owner of record or holder of legal title is one of the following:
1. An agent, nominee, attorney or a person acting in some other capacity on behalf of the U.S. person with respect to the account;
2. A corporation in which the U.S. person owns directly or indirectly, (i) more than 50% of the total value of shares of stock or (ii) more than 50% of the voting power of all shares of stock,
3. A partnership in which the U.S. person owns directly or indirectly: (i) an interest in more than 50% of the partnership's profits or (ii) an interest in more than 50% of the partnership capital,
4. A trust by which the U.S. person: (i) is the trust grantor and (ii) has an ownership interest in the trust for U.S. federal tax purposes;
5. A trust in which the U.S. person has a greater than 50% present beneficial interest in the assets or income of the trust for the calendar year, or
6. Any other entity in which the U.S. person owns directly or indirectly more than 50% of the voting power.

So, most likely, you will need to also include the foreign financial accounts for your business in the required reporting.

Currently, as of the date of writing this book, only individuals are required to file the Form 8938. It is expected that the IRS will change this in the near future to require corporations to also file this form.

You will also need to do reporting for the business structures. Remember this is all just reporting. So far, there is no tax due, or at least we haven't discussed the tax returns necessary when you have tax due from your foreign business.

Foreign Corporations

If you have a foreign corporation, there are two additional tax forms you'll need to file.

U.S. taxpayers, domestic trusts, or domestic corporations must report any transfers to a foreign corporation by filing IRS Form 926. A tax-exempt entity must also file Form 926 if there are transfers to a foreign corporation. If a married couple has a joint transfer, they both must each individually file Form 926.

A U.S. taxpayer who directly or indirectly owns any interest in certain foreign corporations probably will have to file Form 5471. In a minute, I'll go through the categories of who needs to file and when. But, first, let me tell you why it's so important.

When the IRS audits your return under 'normal' circumstances, they do it by disallowing some deductions or trying to change the definition of something you have done on your return. Honestly, most of the time you can negotiate if you've handled it properly from the beginning with an experienced CPA or tax attorney. But, if you fail to file a Form 5471, there is no negotiation. You didn't do what you were required to do. Period.

Form 5471 is a complicated form to file. In fact, it takes 32 hours to complete, according to the IRS instructions. You need to report a lot of information about the foreign corporation including income statements, balance sheet, loans and information on all shareholders. And, most importantly, very few CPAs have experience with the reporting. In fact, most of the standard 'tax organizers' that you might receive from your CPA don't even ask about any offshore holdings. But, make no mistake, if you don't file, you could face a penalty of $10,000 or more and even jail time.

In the past, it has been difficult for the IRS to learn ownership information on foreign corporations. That all changed with FATCA which requires foreign financial institutes to report on any deposits that are someway connected to a U.S. citizen. The IRS is actively involved in gaining more information of US citizens finances overseas, and will only increase its efforts in the future. Additionally, there are an increasing number of U.S-Foreign Government Tax Treaties that require cooperation of the nations with respect to the exchange of tax information.

The IRS requires the filing of a From 5471 for the following group.

A U.S. citizen or resident who is an officer or director of a foreign corporation in which a U.S. person has acquired:

- Stock which meets the 10% stock ownership criteria, or
- An additional 10% or more (in value or voting power) of the outstanding stock of the foreign corporation was added.

A U.S. person who acquires stock, which, without regard to stock already owned on the date of acquisition, meets the 10% stock ownership criteria with respect to the foreign corporation.

A person who is treated as a U.S. shareholder under Section 953 (c) meets the same requirements.

Another group who must file are U.S. persons who had control of a foreign corporation for at least 30 days. Controls is defined as:

1. More than 50% of the total combined voting power of all classes of stock of the foreign corporation or
2. More than 50% of the total value of shares of all classes of stock of the foreign corporation.

That's just the overview. If you have any interest or control in a foreign corporation, plan on needing to file this form and make sure you're working with an experienced tax professional who understands foreign information reports.

Foreign Partnership Reporting

Just like the case of U.S. taxpayers owning or controlling a foreign corporation, U.S. taxpayers also have a reporting requirement if they have or control a foreign partnership.

A person controls a partnership if they hold more than 50 percent of the partnership interest. If no partner has a controlling share, then all partners with more than 10 percent partnership interest must file Form 8865. In addition, U.S. taxpayers who acquire or dispose of partnership interest in a foreign partnership must disclose the transaction to the IRS. Most foreign LLCs with two or more persons are defined as foreign partnership for tax purposes.

U.S. persons that own a controlling interest in a foreign partnership are subject to relatively new reporting requirements.

Additionally, a fairly new provision in Section 6046A of the Internal Revenue Code requires that a U.S. person with an interest in a foreign partnership file Form 8865 when they have a "reportable event" during the tax year.

Reportable events include acquisitions, dispositions and changes in proportional interests for U.S. persons of at least 10%.

This 10% interest change could be a change in the capital interest, change in the profit interest or change in the allocation of deductions and losses. A "person" in this case means U.S. citizens or residents, domestic partnerships and corporations and domestic trusts and estates.

The Form 8865 informational return must contain the following information:

1. The name, address and taxpayer identification number of the U.S. person required to file the return.

2. If the U.S. person is treated as owning an interest in a foreign partnership by application of the attribution rules, information about the foreign and/or domestic persons who actually own the interest in the foreign partnership.
3. Information about all foreign entities that were owned by the foreign partnership.
4. For each reportable event, include the date and type of event, and the U.S. person's direct percentage interest in the foreign partnership immediately before and immediately after the event.
5. The fair market value of the interest that was acquired or was disposed.
6. Information about foreign and domestic partnerships that the foreign partnership owned interests of at least 10% either directly or constructively during the partnership's tax year ending with or within the year of the person filing Form 8865.

Foreign Trust

The third type of foreign entity that may require reporting for a U.S. taxpayer is the foreign trust. There may additionally be tax due. Whether a trust is taxable or not is a little more complicated than the more straightforward, albeit snoopy, information report requirements. We cover foreign trusts in more detail, including some of the myths and mistakes regarding them in Section 4: Investing Offshore.

Domestic or Foreign?

Domestic trusts are subject to U.S. taxation on their worldwide income. Generally, if it is a grantor trust, the grantor will be subject to taxation.

In the case of a non-grantor trust, the trust beneficiaries are subject to tax when income is distributed. Otherwise, the non-grantor trust is subject to taxation for non-distributed income.

A foreign trust, on the other hand, is only subject to U.S. taxation on U.S. source income. This would include income from the active conduct of a U.S. trade or business, interest from U.S. residents of business, dividends from domestic corporations, rentals and royalties from U.S. property and gains from the disposition of U.S. real estate.

A trust is a domestic trust if it meets both of these tests:

1. Court Test: A U.S. court must have authority over the trust. If the trust agreement is governed under the laws of a foreign court, it is a foreign trust, and

2. Control Test: One or more U.S. persons must have the ability to control all substantial decisions of the trust.

If you set up a foreign trust to maintain foreign income, and you are a U.S. citizen or resident, you will have a domestic trust unless the trust document specifically states that a foreign government has jurisdiction.

Grantor or Non-Grantor

The question whether your trust is grantor or non-grantor is important whether you have a domestic trust or foreign trust. Since, we're talking about a foreign trust, that's what we'll focus on.

A foreign grantor trust (as opposed to a foreign non-grantor trust) exists if the trust meets these two conditions:

1. The grantor reserves to the right to revoke the trust solely or with the consent of a related or subordinate party; or

2. The amounts distributable during the life of the grantor are distributable only to the grantor and/or the spouse of the grantor.

In the case of a U.S. owner of a foreign grantor trust, the owner will pay U.S. tax on the trust's worldwide income. If the foreign grantor trust has a foreign owner and invest in U.S. assets, there can be complete avoidance of U.S. tax. A U.S. owner won't get the same avoidance.

If you have a foreign non-grantor trust, you will be subject to additional taxes. This is a complicated type of trust and I strongly urge anyone considering a foreign non-grantor trust to talk to both an attorney and a CPA to make sure you understand the tax impact.

Foreign Non-Grantor Trust

The foreign non-grantor trust (FNGT) used to be set up to save or at least largely avoid U.S. taxes. Or at least, people thought it was. Over the years Congress has closed the tax breaks. In fact, a FNGT can actually have more taxes associated with it than if the trust didn't exist and certainly requires a more complicated (and expensive) tax return.

In the case of a grantor trust, the income is earned by the owner whether or not the income is distributed. Income doesn't compound in the trust, but cash may. That means that the grantor will pay U.S. taxes whether or not he or she receives cash.

In the case of a non-grantor trust, the undistributed income is owned by the trust. Undistributed income in year 1 becomes undistributed net income (UNI) in year 2. This is different from the way a non-grantor domestic trust is treated. So, when it comes to taxes, make sure your tax preparer knows the difference.

The taxable income for the foreign non-grantor trust will receive a deduction equal to DNI (distributable net income). This is taxable income to the beneficiaries. (So, there is no tax savings for the beneficiaries.) But, so far there isn't a big tax issue for the trust either. Hold on, though, the big problem is next.

The FNGT is subject to throwback tax. If there has been undistributed net income that is later distributed, the total amount of distribution is taxable plus an interest charge is calculated. That means you will pay tax on more than you received as a beneficiary of a FNGT. Once a FNGT has UNI it will remain in the trust until is it distributed. Until recently, there were some ways around it, but those loopholes have all been closed. If you have UNI, you will pay more tax than you would have if it had been a grantor trust.

The biggest tax question with a FNGT is what will you do to avoid the UNI. One way is to distribute all DNI within 65 days of year end. Another is to invest in tax-exempt bonds. The tax-exempt income is not included in DNI (and therefore you don't have the issue with distributions of tax-exempt income.)

Probably the most common strategy is to invest a FNGT in private-placement life insurance. The death benefits and policy loans are tax-free and so do not need to be included in DNI.

Bottomline, if you're going to set up a foreign trust, make sure you understand what you need to have to qualify as a grantor trust and if you don't qualify, understand what additional taxes you will need to pay unless you carefully plan.

Any U.S. person who receives directly or indirectly a distribution from a foreign trust must meet certain reporting requirements, even if they are not subject to U.S. tax. It doesn't matter whether the distribution is to a beneficiary. It doesn't matter whether the trust is grantor or non-grantor trust.

A Form 3520 is also required if a U.S. person must report (1) any gift from a non-resident individual or foreign estate that collectively exceed $ 100,000; and (2) any gifts from foreign corporations and foreign partnerships that collectively exceed $10,000 (adjusted for inflation). In calculating the $100,000 threshold, the U.S. person must aggregate gifts from different, foreign nonresident aliens and foreign estates if he or she knows (or has reason to know) that one of those persons is acting as the nominee for the other person.

It is possible to set up foreign entities to protect your assets and reduce your taxes, but you're also going to be filing a lot more tax returns. Weigh the costs carefully and make sure the benefit is worth the extra work and cost.

Form 3520-A must be filed by the trust. This is the annual information return of foreign trusts with a U.S. owner. The trustee of a foreign grantor trust is required to file it. But, if he fails to do so, the penalty will be assessed on the grantor.

There will also likely be a requirement to file the FinCen 114 for deposit balances over $10,000.

And, of course, you will have taxes to pay on your individual income tax return if you are a U.S. taxpayer.

Chapter 13 Review

1. Do you have a plan in place to compile the information needed to file the individual reporting requirements?
2. Is your current CPA up-to-date on the filing requirements?
3. As you plan your business structures, are you aware of the filing requirements and cost to file returns for and maintain these structures?

Section Three: Retire Internationally

Intro to Section Three

Have you ever thought of retiring offshore? Maybe you thought it was just a dream to live in a cosmopolitan city or a secluded beach paradise. It's an exciting prospect, but there are a lot of doubts and concerns that might creep in. For example, maybe you've thought these things and that's what is stopping you from retiring overseas.

"I can't afford it."

That may be true, depending on where you choose to move. There are inexpensive options, though. For example, it is possible to live on as little as $1,200 per month in places like Panama, Columbia, Thailand, Nicaragua, and Malaysia.

Don't assume how much it may cost. Find out for yourself!

"It's not the right time."

If you're waiting for the economy to change, to have more certainty about living in the new country or are using some other reason to delay your decision, chances are it will never be the right time.

Richard and I have lived outside the U.S. twice. Thinking back, I'm sure it wasn't the right time. Because, after all, when is the right time? We could have definitely have just stayed where we were here in the U.S. But as a result of moving when we did, we learned a new language, a new culture and created memories to last forever.

We're back in the U.S., but I don't think we will stay here forever. There is just too much adventure out there!

How about you? If you feel drawn to retire offshore, but are thinking it's not the time right now, when will it be right?

"I don't have enough money for retirement. I need to earn extra income."

In today's world, with a little imagination and self-confidence, you can earn a little income anywhere. You may become a worker in a foreign company, maybe start your own business or work online.

I noticed the other day that the city of Rosarito, where we had lived in Mexico, was now soliciting Americans to start businesses. They are even providing start-up grants for Americans to start businesses to provide goods and services to other expat Americans. I think it's part of an overall plan to attract a growing foreign population.

It can be easier today for an American to earn an independent living in a foreign country than in the United States, because you have knowledge, experience, skills, and connections that the locals don't. Plus, if you've ever lived out of the U.S., you know what it is like to miss certain things. It could be food items, household gadgets or even a particular type of tea, like my favorite Irish breakfast tea. There can be a good business providing those goods to other expats.

"I don't have enough capital to make an international move like this."

You might be surprised how inexpensive it can be to actually move. You probably will find that you have to look at the things you've accumulated with a more jaded eye. What is worth storing? What is worth shipping? And what is it that you really don't need or want anymore? It's possible to move with your pets. In fact, it is actually easier than you might realize.

"I don't speak the language."

It's such a wonderful opportunity to learn! I'm a strong believer in learning a second language. It expands your horizons and your ability to communicate. But even if learning a language is the last thing you want to do, you're still lucky. English is the world's language. It's how we do business globally.

"I'm too old."

As you get older, chances are you'll need more care. And, that is often much cheaper as well as more reliable in other countries.

Besides there is something to be said about you're just as old as you feel. Sometimes a move with the new adventure is just what you need.

In 2009, I had a tough decision. We were living in Baja California at the beach (in Mexico) and my husband, Richard, was diagnosed with swine flu. The doctors in Mexico had the necessary medicine there and could treat him, but they asked if I would rather get an ambulance to take Richard to San Diego, CA. I called the U.S. hospital and found that they did not have the medicine. There was a shortage. They said to bring Richard, but I had to also bring medicine to treat him. Plus, they said they were going to put him in strict quarantine.

I made the decision to keep Richard in Mexico. His temperature was so high that he couldn't make any logical decisions. So it was mine to make and I really was afraid that I would make the wrong one. The hospital got us a nurse who specialized in homeopathy and natural treatments to build up his immune system and especially his liver. He kept on the medicine for Swine Flu. He got through it alive and with no side effects.

We don't always think of Latin America for quality medical treatment, but the fact is that the society, in general, has a more nurturing and caring culture. I think that's what saved my husband's life.

"I've got to wait for my children to finish school."

This can be a hard one for a lot of people, but the reality is that traveling, learning another language, another culture and history could be the best education your children could experience.

I think the final word for deciding whether to move or retire offshore is what is best for you. Is there still adventure in your heart? Are you the kind of person who can roll with what happens, accepting of the beauty in difference and love the idea of being free, than maybe retiring offshore is for you.

Making the Move Offshore to Panama

Debbie Fishell, originally from Phoenix, AZ, and her husband recently made to move to Panama. Here's their story.

People make a decision to leave their home country and relocate abroad for a multitude of reasons. In my case, the reasons I chose are very common among other North Americans that I talk to. I was sick of the intrusion from the IRS and its ever increasing taxes (especially after 4 years of audits on my personal and business returns - ALL with no changes!) and fear of the downward direction the government is taking the country in so many ways. After a great deal of research, my husband and I chose Panama as our new home. Panama is a secure democratic country that is moving forward in a positive direction.

Making the move to Panama turned out to be a lot easier than we thought. The Panamanian government actually wants foreigners to come here! They realize the benefit in the added commerce and spending that comes with new residents. This may be one of the factors that contributed to the GDP of Panama, which averaged 9 Percent from 2010 until 2014. There are numerous incentives for business owners and retirees that attract us to this diverse little country. It's easy to visit Panama from most countries, just show your passport at the airport, get a stamp, and you can stay in the country for 180 days.

Two of the most popular forms of residency in Panama are the "Pensianado Visa" and the "Friendly Nations" visa. The first is available to any foreigner who collects a pension of $1000 (+ $250 for a spouse) from a government or company. Social Security qualifies and there are many discounts for a pensioner in Panama, on everything from transportation to utility bills and medical costs. The second requires opening a bank account in Panama of at least $5000 (+ $2000 for a spouse) or buying real estate valued at $100,000 or more. Since we are not collecting a pension yet, we chose the Friendly Nations Visa. There are another dozen or so options for residency and most don't even require you to be in country for a minimum amount of time each year. There are reputable lawyers in Panama that walked us through the process for a reasonable fee. Lawyers in Panama usually have a flat rate for services rather than charging by the hour, or minute. Another perk – Panama is NOT a litigious society. You are lucky to find more than one lawyer in a town outside of Panama City!

There is already a large "expat" population in Panama and its growing. In fact, an attorney recently told me that more people applied for citizenship in Panama in the first quarter of 2014 than in any entire year in the past. This speaks volumes! Especially since you have to be a resident for 5 years before applying to become a citizen. The nice thing about a large number of gringos being here, who have paved the way through their moving to Panama, is that relocation information is available for the asking. I learned a lot through joining various online forums around the country.

When it came time to make our move we accomplished it in 2 fairly easy trips. The house was purchased using an attorney, with no realtor involved. It cost less than half of a comparable home in Phoenix.

We decided not to bring most of our household items because everything is available here in Panama. Most things can be replaced for the cost of shipping, so why not get new? Some valuables, like my grandmother's china, are in storage with our daughter for now, or maybe forever. My husband did not want to part with his restored 1979 VW Van, so he loaded it up with his tools and a few of our personal things and drove from Arizona to Panama. This turned out to be quite an adventure and he says he would not recommend it. The cost was high and the trip fraught with stress. I sold my car and purchased a vehicle in Panama, which was much easier. Full coverage insurance only cost me $240 for a whole year! When I flew to Panama for the final step in our move, I had my two small dogs in tow. There was a precise set of instructions and paperwork online required to get them into Panama. Funny, it is more difficult to get a dog into the country than a person! It cost about $600 per dog for everything, including vet expenses, airline carriers, and fees. They seem to like their new home with a new adventure every day.

We left all of our furniture and opted for new since everything we need is readily available in Panama and it is cheaper than shipping. Utilities and high speed Internet were hooked up with the help of an interpreter at $10 per hour. Total utility bill for our first month in Panama, everything included, was less than $50!

What cannot be purchased, and is the best part of living in our new home in Panama, is the genuine friendliness of the people here. Pretty much everyone that I pass on the street says "buenas", with a smile, and they are happy to work through my sign language as I learn to perfect my use of Spanish. People here appear to be more accountable for their actions rather than having signs posted everywhere telling them what to do or not do. Then there's the new feeling of "tranquilo" because no one in Panama is in a hurry. You can check out more about other Panama adventures at www.EscapeArtist.com/Panama or through Facebook at www.Facebook.com/PanamaEscapeArtist.

Are you ready for your adventure?

Chapter 14: Five Things to Do Before You Retire Internationally

Are you ready to retire offshore? There can be financial and tax advantages to leaving in the right way. On the other hand, if you miss a few steps you can find yourself never escaping state tax and having your pension and disability payments slashed. Here are five things to consider before you leave the U.S.

#1: Is It Time To Change Your State?

Is the state you are moving from going to cause a problem later?

Some U.S. states continue to collect state income tax even after you have moved out of the country. For example, if you are moving abroad from California, South Carolina, New Mexico or Virginia, the state will continue to chase you for income tax returns and state tax even after you've moved out. The best solution if you're from one of these states or are concerned your current home state may be considering the same onerous tax burden is to move to a state with no state income tax. The most common states to move to are Nevada, Florida or Texas.

Changing your state of residence can be tricky, though. If you've lived in a state for a long time, obviously, your residence is easier to prove. But if you decide to move from California to Nevada shortly before you move out of the country, residency can be a little more subjective.

Following is a checklist of items to do that can help you prove you had residency in another state prior to your move.

- Purchase or lease a residence in new state,
- Move household items to the new home,
- File a homestead exemption in the new state,
- Register for school with the new address,
- Get driver's license in the new state,

- Register cars in the new state,
- Open new bank account & safe deposit box in the new state,
- Change address on credit cards,
- Register to vote in the new state,
- File federal tax return with new address,
- Refer to the new address on all legal and trust documents
- Create a religious affiliation in new state, if applicable
- Enroll children in sports and other classes in the new state,
- Change your passport address to the new state, and
- Join other organizations in your new state.

The point is to be able to demonstrate that you really did make a new residence in another state prior to leaving the U.S.

#2: Is Your Money Going With You?

Part of the move will obviously include your investments. Here are some things to consider:

- Which currency will you use for your cash assets?
- Do you have a foreign bank picked out?
- Have you found the best way to exchange currencies?
- Will you get an offshore credit card?
- Make sure your CPA is familiar with international tax laws and knows which disclosures you are required to make. Will you need to file in your new country as well?

#3: Is Your Asset Protection In Place?

Asset protection plans actually require an on-going procedure. Things change and your plans need to stay up to date. Consider who your potential creditors could be. Do you have IRS issues? This is a case where you need to maintain contact with a U.S. CPA or attorney with experience in asset protection to fully utilize the unique benefits available when you move out of the U.S.

#4: How Will Moving Outside the Country Impact Your Financial Goals?

Along with the asset protection, you'll also want to consider your financial goals. What is your plan when you are outside the country? You can get great tax breaks for income that does not have nexus in the U.S., but you need to consider your assets in the U.S. first. How will you liquidate them with the least amount of tax?

#5: How Will You Manage Your Finances Across Countries?

Some of the things to consider when you move into another country

- Security for your important documents,
- Quick access to these documents, and
- Ability to get current bank and investment values.

There is a lot to consider when you move out of the U.S. We've touched on just a few of the financial, legal and tax issues to consider. Probably the biggest thing to consider is to make sure you have an expert in U.S. tax issues abroad. This is a unique part of tax law and few CPAs have the experience and education in this niched market. Make sure you're getting the best advice you can.

Chapter 14 Review:

1. After reviewing these five steps, to which do you need to pay special attention?
2. If you need to move to another state, are you able to meet all of the requirements to legitimately establish residency in another state? If not, which ones could be a problem for you?
3. Have you considered what changes this may make to your investment strategies, asset protection and financial goals?

4. Do you have U.S. advisors (CPA and attorney) that understand the financial, asset protection and tax tricks and traps of moving offshore?

Chapter 15: Receiving Social Security Benefits While Living Abroad

One of the biggest questions that needs to be answered before retirees are ready to the leave the U.S. has to do with Social Security and SS Disability payments.

Can You Receive Social Security Benefits While Outside the U.S.?

If you are a U.S. citizen, you may receive Social Security (SS) outside the U.S. as long as you are eligible. Part of that eligibility has to do with which country you are in. Currently, the following countries are approved for foreign resident U.S. citizens to still receive SS checks:

Austria, Belgium, Canada, Chile, Czech Republic, Finland, France, Germany, Greece, Ireland, Israel, Italy, Japan, Korea (South), Luxembourg, Netherlands, Norway, Poland, Portugal, Spain, Sweden, Switzerland and United Kingdom.

If you are a citizen of one of the countries below, you are still eligible unless you are receiving your payments as a dependent or survivor:

Albania, Antigua and Barbuda, Argentina, Bahama Islands, Barbados, Belize, Bolivia, Bosnia-Herzegovina, Bulgaria, Brazil, Burkina Faso, Columbia, Costa Rica, Cote d'Ivoire, Croatia, Cyprus, Dominica, Dominican Republic, Ecuador, El Salvador, Gabon, Grenada, Guatemala, Guyana, Hungary, Iceland, Jamaica, Jordan, Latvia, Liechtenstein, Lithuania, Macedonia, Malta, Marshall Islands, Mexico, Micronesia, Monaco, Montenegro, Nicaragua, Palau, Panama, Peru, Philippines, Romania, St. Kitts and Nevis, St. Lucia, St. Vincent and the Grenadines, Samoa, San Marino, Serbia, Slovakia, Slovenia, Trinidad-Tobago, Turkey, Uruguay and Venezuela.

If you are not a U.S. citizen or a citizen of the countries in the first list, the SS payments will stop once you have been outside the U.S. for 6 months unless:

- You were eligible for SS benefit since December, 1956,
- You are in active military service, or
- You had been a railroad worker.

It gets more complicated if you have children who are receiving SS. The best bet is to talk to your financial planner or CPA as part of your moving offshore strategy.

Can You Receive Disability Payments if You Move Offshore?

There are two types of disability payments you may be receiving from Social Security. These are Social Security Disability Insurance payments (SSDI) or Supplemental Security Income payments (SSI). In one case, the disability payments will continue. And in the other, the payments stop 30 days after you leave the U.S..

SSDI:

If you are a U.S. citizen, you are able to receive your disability benefits as long as it is SSDI and you have moved to an allowed country. The disallowed countries include Cuba, North Korea, Cambodia, Vietnam and most of the former Soviet Union.

If you are a U.S. legal resident, but not a citizen, your SSDI benefits will stop after 6 months.

You may need to come back to the U.S. periodically for reviews.

SSI:

If your disability payments are based on Supplemental Security Income (SSI), your payments will stop once you leave the U.S. for 30 days. There are a few possible exceptions:

- Children of military personnel who receive SSI who have to leave when parents leave will still receive SSI disability.

- The U.S. includes the Northern Mariana islands, but does not include Puerto Rico.

Contact your CPA before you move to make sure you understand your rights to SS and/or disability payments. The rules are complicated and payment will depend on the type of benefits you have and the country to which you're moving.

Chapter 15 Review:

1. If you currently receive Social Security payments, check to see what agreements are in place in the country you intend to move to. Will you be able to continue to receive the payments?
2. Next, determine if your payments are based on income you earned or whether these come as part of SSI. Will your payments be reduced if you move offshore?

Chapter 16: Pension Conversion When You're Offshore

One of the conversations I frequently have with clients who are considering retirement is what do they intend to do with their pension accounts. This actually can be a conversation that could happen for anyone when they have a downturn in taxable income.

A move offshore can provide a unique opportunity for tax planning. If you still work, and can qualify for the foreign earned income exclusion and housing allowance as discussed in Chapter 4, your taxable income will drop. And that's the perfect time for a pension conversion, which sets you up for little or no tax for the rest of your life from your pension.

Let's take a step back and go through this point-by-point.

First of all, let's look at the difference between a regular pension plan and a Roth plan.

Roth Account

Contributions to Roth accounts are not tax deductible in the year of the contribution. So, there is no tax deduction. However, the money they make is 100% tax free. There is no tax when you pull it out in the form of distributions.

In contrast, contributions to other traditional retirement accounts (401ks, IRAs, etc.) are tax deductible. The plans grow tax-deferred, so there is no immediate tax due. However, the distributions will be fully taxable.

If your income is high, the tax-deductible regular pension is a good idea. But, there is the problem of tax later down the road, when you take the distributions.

And the investments aren't growing tax-free, it's just tax-deferred income if you have a regular pension. That's where a pension conversion strategy comes into play.

Pension Conversion Strategy

The Pension Conversion Strategy takes advantage of a low income year to convert a regular pension into a Roth. You pay tax based on the value of the conversion at the time of the conversion. The ideal situation would be to convert when your income is lower and the pension value is lower, usually because investments have dropped in value.

In this case, though, regardless of whether the value of the investments have gone down, you still can make use of the great tax breaks to have lower taxable income. That means when you convert some or all of your pension to a Roth, you will be doing so at a lower tax bracket. That's because you presumably have been able to take advantage of foreign earned income exclusion.

There is one more reason to do that after you move offshore: state income taxes.

If you live offshore when you make the conversion, there will be no state tax. And, then, later if you move back to the U.S., you will never have to pay state income tax on the pension. You have paid federal tax, after a fashion, because the conversion will be subject to federal tax.

This is just one of the many tax strategies you can use when you move offshore. Let's go over this particular strategy, in bullet form.

- Move offshore, making sure you have taken steps to ensure that state tax doesn't continue to follow you.
- Option: Use foreign earned income tax exclusion and housing deduction to reduce your taxable income.
- Convert some or all of your regular tax-deferred pension to a tax-free Roth.
- You'll pay federal tax on the conversion amount, but at a lower federal tax rate and with no state tax.

This actually could be a strategy for someone who has a lot of pension to convert. Move offshore for a few years!

Chapter 16 Review:

1. If you have a pension plan, have you discussed this plan with your CPA? Does it make sense to convert some or all of it to a Roth?

Chapter 17: Should You Have an Offshore Pension Plan?

If you live offshore, or are considering a move offshore, at some time you'll probably be approached about an offshore pension or offshore savings plan. Like any other investment scheme, you'll see promotional material with graphs showing possible growth scenarios. The key, of course, is the word "possible." Due diligence will often disclose what the assumptions of return and the fees will be. It's up to you to determine how realistic those assumptions will be.

When it comes to offshore pension or investment plans, I'm neutral. Some work. Some don't. But, there are definitely things that you need to consider.

Here are some general things to consider before you set up an offshore investment plan.

A pension plan or a life insurance investment plan is only as good as the underlying investments. Just like the plans that I see pitched to my U.S. clients now and then, a foreign investment plan, no matter what the particular tax vehicle, really depends on the investments to make money. Buying a whole life insurance policy might be a good idea and might be a horrible idea. The insurance often has nothing to do with the investments. The same is true with setting up an offshore pension plan. If you're planning to make more money with it, that would be because of the investments, not the plan.

Watch the fees. If you have an investment, you're probably going to pay some kind of fees. If you wrap it in an insurance company or annuity, you're going to pay some kind of fees. If you do all of this through an offshore entity, you're going to have more fees. The point here is to make sure you know how much you are paying and that the benefits you receive are worth the cost.

Make sure you understand U.S. tax implications. Of course, you will have reporting requirements as we've discussed previously in this book. But, you also may face some high taxes if the investment qualifies as a Passive Foreign Investment Company (PFIC). The IRS has issued some new reporting requirements for PFIC shareholders. Make sure your CPA is aware of the changes.

A non-US corporation is generally a PFIC if:

1. 75% or more of its gross income for the taxable year is passive income or
2. The average percentage of assets it holds during the taxable year,

which produce passive income or which are held for the production of passive income is at least 50%.

If a U.S. investor holds shares in such a company there are special federal income tax and reporting rules. The tax rules are complicated and detailed. Without going into all of the detailed and complicated rules, the summary is simply that the goal is to deny the potential deferral of U.S. tax that might otherwise be available to a U.S. person that invests in a foreign investment fund that accumulates income. The PFIC rules effectively force U.S. shareholders in a PFIC, no matter how small the investment, to recognize income earned by the PFIC currently or else pay U.S. tax at the highest possible rate plus interest on the income once it is distributed.

A single share of stock in a PFIC is enough to subject a shareholder to the PFIC rules and a person can be a PFIC shareholder through indirect ownership. All of this means you may have additional tax returns to file and probably some unexpected taxes to pay.

Chapter 17 Review:

1. Do you have a team together that you trust to advise you on the best business structures and investment opportunities?

2. If you do decide to establish an offshore pension plan, do you have a CPA who is experienced with the required filings and are you prepared to pay the higher fees to file additional returns?

Section Four: Invest Abroad

Introduction to Section Four

Many Americans are thinking globally these days. It might mean moving offshore, working offshore, moving a business offshore or, like we're going to discuss in this section, investing offshore.

Investing might be as simple as setting up an international bank account. When we lived in another country, we had U.S. bank accounts and an international account through HSBC. That's just one of the international banking options. Another one is Citibank. In the case of HSBC and Citibank, they are really promoting an international investment and bank account.

By setting up with one of the big global banks, you will have access to different types of investments or other financial products than you might normally find in just one country. You can manage your bank account anywhere in the world. When you move offshore, you'll find that you need to have that access and ability to convert currencies.

We do need to clear up one possible 'benefit.' That so-called benefit has to do with hiding income from the IRS. You can't do it. You have to pay tax on income that the IRS recognizes. But, that doesn't mean you necessarily have to disclose everything.

And, that legal loophole is one that you need to consider when you make offshore investments.

If you are a U.S. citizen or resident, or a foreign national with a green card, you will need to report on most of your offshore investments.

We've talked about them several times in this book, but just to refresh your memory, the three separate reporting requirements are:

1. You must file if you have over $10,000 in a foreign financial account at any time in the year. That is done on Form FinCen 114 and must be filed by June 30th. If you don't file it by then, you face a huge penalty.

2. You must report that you have foreign financial account on your Schedule B of your regular Form 1040 income tax return.
3. If you meet other reporting thresholds ($75,000 at any time during the year or $50,000 at the end of the year if you're single), you need to also file Form 8938.

But, there are some things you don't need to report.
1. Precious metals. If you hold gold, silver or other precious metals outside the U.S. these do not need to be reported to the IRS.
2. Real estate. Direct ownership of real estate in your own name is not reportable. But, if you the rent the property out, you are required to report the income.

It may be the time to start looking to offshore investments. You may be able to gain reduced portfolio risk through global and currency diversification, increased privacy and a financial lifeboat for your family.

Chapter 18: Basics of International Investing

You might have heard about international investing and, if nothing else, you just read about it the introduction to this section. Before we jump into some the more sophisticated offshore investment vehicles, let's go back and look at some of the basics.

What is International Investing?

There are many different ways you could invest internationally. You may invest through mutual funds, U.S.-traded foreign stocks or by making a direct investment in foreign markets.

The world is becoming more financially integrated. In fact, you might already be invested in foreign markets through your U.S. investments. One quick way to check that out is to look at your year-end statement from your brokerage. If you receive a foreign tax credit, you've got foreign investments. Make sure your tax preparer is giving you credit for those foreign taxes that were paid on your behalf.

There can be a big surprise to an investor who is considering an investment in foreign markets, and thinking that it will be complicated. You don't necessarily need to set up a foreign entity to hold foreign investments. If your purpose is to diversify your investments, you can do it right now, while you're living in the U.S.

It used to be that people associated offshore investments with illegal tax evasion or hiding money away for nefarious reasons. Most of the schemes were, at best, marginally legal, but that has all changed.

In July, 2014, the Foreign Account Tax Compliance Act came into full force. This requires foreign financial institutes to provide information about investments held by U.S. citizens, residents or those who are legally working in the U.S.

The two main legal reasons that people want to invest outside the U.S. are:

1. Diversification. You spread your investment risk among foreign companies and markets that are different than the U.S. economy, and
2. Growth. You can take advantage of growth in other markets, particularly those of emerging nations. The U.S. is just finally recovering from the Great Recession, but there are countries around the world that never had a recession. In fact, they are moving faster and making great strides economically.

There can also be more risk with international investments. It's important to take a moment here and talk about the difference between a tax or asset protection device and the underlying investment. It's a question I'll get through my CPA firm every now and then. Someone is asking me whether it's a good investment to have a foreign trust or maybe a foreign foundation. The answer is always the same. I have no idea.

That's because if you're looking for the value of an investment, then you need to look at the investment. The structure will help you with asset protection and possibly tax savings, but it won't help you get a better return or reduce risk.

There are additionally special risks with international investing.

1. Currency trading risk. When the currency exchange rate changes between the U.S. Dollar (USD) and the foreign currency, your investment value will change, too. So, not only do you need to pay attention to the investment itself, you also need to pay attention to currency rates.
2. Bigger fluctuations. You'll have larger market fluctuations because you're not only dealing with investment risk, but also national and currency risk.
3. Political and social change. If you are investing outside the country, you may not be as aware of changes inside that country.

4. Liquidity. An investment in a foreign market will probably be less liquid. If you need your cash, how easy will it be to sell the investment?

If I were to say there was one thing I wanted everyone to take away from this chapter, it would be the need to think about offshore investments as investments. In the next few chapters, we're going to talk about a couple of foreign structures that are popular for some in the offshore investment field. An offshore investment is only as good as the investment itself.

Chapter 18 Review

1. What is your goal for your international investments?
2. How do you plan to counter the four international investment risks?

Chapter 19: Foreign Trust Myths and Mistakes

The foreign trust is a sophisticated tax and asset protection planning device. There are a lot of myths and misunderstanding about what a foreign trust can do. The foreign trust does not make you completely bulletproof. And, the foreign trust will need to be reported to the IRS if a U.S. person is involved.

The foreign trust is only as strong as the laws of the jurisdiction in which the trust is established. So, picking the right country is important. Plus, if the assets of a foreign trust are still in the U.S., a U.S. court will have jurisdiction on the assets. Make sure you pick the right country for your foreign trust, if you and your advisor decide that is the best plan for you. And, make sure you carry through with the transfer of assets if you want the foreign trust to hold all assets with the foreign country's asset protection benefits.

A foreign trust in the right jurisdiction will insulate assets from usual commercial and civil tort claims, matrimonial claims, forced inheritance and even civil government actions. The foreign trust provides another general benefit. A future creditor will discover that he is faced with expensive litigation if he proceeds with a claim. So, the creditor will generally settle a case rather than fight it.

4 Steps to a Foreign Trust

Just like any other part of your tax-saving, asset-protecting strategy, there are some steps you need to take first.

1. What jurisdiction will you use? Some of the considerations are how solid the laws are, what are possible tax considerations and what is the economic and political stability of the area. "Foreign" doesn't necessarily mean better than what you already have in the U.S. I recommend that you have an experienced advisor helping you choose the right jurisdiction.

2. What are the legal precedents in the jurisdiction? Again, you need an experienced advisor helping you. That's because he or

she will have experience with different jurisdictions. They'll know the friendly places to park your foreign trust. If you don't have solid, legal precedents, you may find that you foreign trust won't stand up if you get a claim against the assets. You want to see what the choice of law provisions are available, the treats and policies with respect to foreign judgment and the tax structure in that country.

3. Does the country have enough technology to provide easy communication and distance banking? And, since the implementation of FATCA (Foreign Account Tax Compliance Act) on July 1, 2014, we also need to look at what has happened with local banking. Some banks will not allow accounts to be opened if U.S. citizens are involved in any capacity.

4. What is the standard of operation in the country? Some countries are known for corruption within the government and judicial process. Those areas should be avoided!

The IRS has recently come down hard on abusive foreign trust arrangements. In fact, this has been one of the dirty dozen audit targets for a few years. An abusive trust arrangement is any trust scheme which purports to reduce or eliminate federal income taxes in ways that are not permitted by federal tax law. Abusive trust arrangements are typically promoted by the promise of tax benefits with no change in the taxpayer's control over or benefit from the taxpayer's former income or assets.

The IRS has a task force to closely scrutinize trust schemes, both domestic and foreign. And, at the same time, many tax haven jurisdictions participate in the new exchange of tax information treaties with the U.S.

None of this should concern or scare you, though, if you intend to follow the reporting laws and you have an experienced tax professional keeping you in compliance.

We discussed foreign grantor trusts and foreign non-grantor trusts in Chapter 12 in detail regarding the tax reporting and income taxability concerns. Let's take a second and talk about why you might use one and not the other.

A foreign grantor trust means that all of the income will flow through to you. Taxes may be a little higher and you'll definitely have more costs to set up and maintain the foreign trust. The main reason why people use foreign grantor trusts is for asset protection.

A foreign non-grantor trust has a more complicated tax situation. If you don't distribute all of the income to the beneficiaries, the income stays in the trust. The undistributed income is then subject to interest, so that when the amount is finally distributed, the taxable income is actually higher than the distribution.

There are a few strategies around that overstated tax. One is to make sure you always distribute the income. If that's the case, the non-grantor trust is more similar to a grantor trust. It's just more complicated.

The other strategy is to make sure the investments within the foreign non-grantor trust don't have taxable income. You might instead invest in tax-exempt bonds or life insurance policies.

We have discussed, in general, the reporting requirements for foreign trusts before, but it's good to go over these again because the penalties are so stiff if you miss a filing.

Trust Reporting Requirements

First, let's start with some definitions that you'll need in order to determine what reporting rules will apply to you. A U.S. person is:

- A citizen or resident of the United States,
- A domestic partnership,
- A domestic corporation,
- Any estate (other than a foreign estate, and

- Any trust if: A court within the U.S. is able to exercise jurisdiction over the trust, and/or one or more U.S. persons have the authority to control all substantial decisions of the trust.

A reportable event is:

- The creation, by a U.S. person, of any foreign trust,
- The transfer of any money or property by a foreign person, including transfer by reason of death to a U.S. person, and
- The death of a citizen or resident of the U.S. if:

1. Decedent was treated as the owner of any portion of a foreign trust, or
2. Any portion of a foreign trust was included in the gross estate of the decedent.

Also, fair market sales and transfers to deferred compensation and charitable trusts are considered reportable events.

Form 3520 is used to report all transactions with foreign trusts and receipt of foreign gifts. This Form should be filed with the taxpayer's annual income tax return. A copy of Form 3520 must also be sent to the Philadelphia Service Center at the same time.

Reporting Requirements for Owners

The owner of any portion of a foreign trust is required to file a return each year which sets forth a full and complete accounting of all trust activities and operations for the year and the name of the U.S. agent for the trust. The owner is also required to report this information to each owner of any portion of the trust or who receives any distribution from the trust.

The Form 3520-A, Annual Information of Foreign Trust with a U.S. Owner, is used to report this information. Now, here is the tricky party. Most of the time this falls to the Trustee to prepare this form.

However, if the Trustee does not make the required report, the U.S. owner will be penalized.

Reporting Requirements for Beneficiaries

Even if you aren't a responsible party or owner of a foreign trust, you may still be responsible for reporting. If you are a beneficiary of a foreign trust who receives any distribution from the foreign trust during the taxable year, you must file information that includes:

1. The name of the trust, and
2. The aggregate amount of the distributions received.

The IRS defines a beneficiary as any person that could possibly benefit, either directly or indirectly, from the trust at any time. That even includes people who are not mentioned in the trust as beneficiaries or people who will be beneficiaries as soon as an amendment to the trust is completed.

Foreign trusts can provide great benefits for U.S. taxpayers, but you have to use them in the right way and for the right purpose. You also need to make sure you're doing all of the reporting.

Chapter 19 Review

1. An investment plan should always start with the investment, not the entity. What type of investment are you considering?
2. What benefit are seeking from a foreign trust?
3. Will it be a grantor or non-grantor trust?

Chapter 20: Should You Have an Offshore Foundation?

Another common tax planning and asset protection idea is to set up an Offshore Foundation. Unlike trusts, private interest foundations have existed for centuries (actually since the Middle Ages) when they were first used for charitable purposes.

Probably the most common offshore foundation, or at least the most prominent, is the Panama Private Interest Foundation. So, let's start there. If the foundation has only foreign interests, then obviously the IRS has nothing to say about the entity. However, if U.S. persons or business entities are founders, investors, grantors or beneficiaries, than the U.S. does have legal jurisdiction.

Since I'm sure someone will send me an article at www.TheOffshoreTaxGuide.com proving that the U.S. does not have jurisdiction over a Panamanian company, let me address that right now. You're absolutely right. The IRS can't tax a foreign company. But they can require reporting and the payment of taxes from U.S. persons and entities. If you, as a U.S. taxpayer, have any connection to a foreign company, you will have U.S. reporting and tax obligations. Period.

A foreign foundation will be treated by the U.S. tax system as a foreign corporation, a foreign trust or a foreign charity. If the entity has a grantor and beneficiaries like a trust, it will be treated as a trust. If it has shareholders, a board of directors and other corporation structures, it will be treated as a foreign corporation. If it is like a charitable institution, it will be treated as a foreign charity.

If the foreign foundation acts like a trust, follow the rules for reporting a foreign trust. That means the grantor will need to file Form 3520, Form 3520-A and the FinCen 114, at a minimum. You can review these rules in Chapter 13.

If the foreign foundation acts like a corporation, follow the rules for reporting like a foreign corporation. That means you'll have to file, at a minimum Form 5471, Form 926 and FinCen 114. You can review the rules for foreign corporations in Chapter 13.

We haven't talked about the special rules for foreign charities; so let's discuss them here.

Foreign organizations that are private foundations and have been granted tax-exempt status are required to pay a 4% excise tax based on their gross investment income received from U.S. sources. If there is a treaty between the U.S. and the foreign country, there may be an exemption or reduction of that amount.

Foreign foundations receiving 85% or more of their support from outside the U.S. are not subject to the same requirements as others such as self-dealing, failure to distribute income, excess business holdings, investments that jeopardize charitable status and taxable expenditures.

A foreign foundation can have its exempt status terminated by the U.S. for repeatedly engaging in prohibited transactions.

Foundations and U.S. Tax

Although I talked about it briefly above, I want to reiterate. If a U.S. person is connected in any way with a foundation, there is a reporting requirement. You might not be required to pay tax, especially if you did not bring any money back into the U.S. and your foundation acts like a grantor trust, but you will still be required to report. If you fail to do so, the penalties are huge and may even include criminal charges and jail!

Chapter 20 Review

1. If you are considering a foreign foundation, how do you intend for it to be treated (corporation, trust or charity)?
2. What will you do with this foundation?

3. Have you discussed your plans with a CPA who is experienced in international tax law?

Section Five: Next Steps

Chapter 21: 5 Steps to Designing Your International Tax Strategy

We recommend that you follow these 5 steps when designing your international tax strategy. These are the same 5 steps whether you are planning to move internationally, invest out of the country, retire out offshore and/or establish a business offshore.

1. Find the right CPA or tax attorney and international specialist.
2. Determine both your immediate and long-term strategy.
3. Lay out the steps to implement your strategy now.
4. Know your reporting responsibilities and have an experienced CPA on board to make the filings.
5. If you find out that you've missed some filings, make sure you catch them up in the right way.

Don't be afraid of offshore tax strategies, but on the other hand, don't just jump into them without having the right U.S. tax expert with you.

When it Goes Wrong

Meet Carl Zwerner. He's an 87 year-old Florida resident who goofed, and a federal jury found him guilty. He's lucky he isn't spending the rest of his life in jail. They had mercy, though, and said he had to pay $2.24 million in penalties. Of course, the fact that he never had more than $1.55 million in his accounts didn't matter. It also didn't matter that he had hired a tax attorney who was supposed to catch up his past unfiled reports. The attorney had made one big mistake, and Mr. Zwerner was going to pay the price.

The problem was that Mr. Zwerner had moved money to Swiss bank accounts. You know, the ones that were supposed to be secret forever. As a result, he didn't file the required reports from 2004-2007. In 2008, he found out he had missed the filings.

One thing that really played against him was that he had completed the annual tax organizer for his CPA by answering "no" to the question that asked, "Do you have an interest in or signature authority over a financial account n a foreign country, such as a bank account, securities account or other financial account?"

His answer in court was that since he held the money in a foundation, he thought that neither the account nor its income was reportable. But, according to the IRS, the use of an offshore entity to hold an unreported foreign account is an attempt at fraud. The jury agreed.

But, there still more to the story. When Zwerner realized that he had missed the filing, he attempted to do a voluntary disclosure in 2008. This was before the IRS had started its formal "Offshore Voluntary Disclosure Program." That meant he would have avoided criminal penalties, but still had to pay the cash penalties.

He attempted to enter to later enter the voluntary disclosure program, but it was after the IRS had already begun its audit of his assets.

In the end, Mr. Zwerner received multiple-year 50% penalties on a single account.

Probably the worst thing about a verdict like this is that the IRS has learned they can really come down hard on someone who doesn't report. The irony, of course, is that the whole issue was with reporting. If he had filed like he should have, he wouldn't have paid a dime in tax. Now he owes more than the accounts ever held.

Step One: Find the Right Advisors

You need a small team of advisors to help you set up an effective offshore tax strategy. If you're going to set up international entities, you will need an international specialist. You'll have U.S. reporting for most assets you hold outside the U.S. and so that means you'll need to have a CPA familiar with the required tax and report implications. You may additionally need a U.S. lawyer to help with the business structures and asset protection in the U.S.

I'm not exactly objective because I see what happens when people fail to follow the U.S. tax rules and so I believe U.S. tax planning is one of the most important aspects of a well-thought-out offshore plan.

The most important part of working with a group of advisors is to make sure that no one crosses over the line of what they should advise on. I can tell you why I like working in Anguilla, but that doesn't mean that Panama won't work for you. It's just coming from the perspective of the cases I've worked on. By the same token, I don't think a non-tax professional should ever advise on tax matters. I especially dislike the crazy advice given by people with no experience who then say that CPAs don't know this secret. Without a doubt, international tax is a specialty and not every CPA will want to work in this area, but there are trained tax professionals. And there is no tax secret that only some offshore business promoter knows that no one else knows.

If you have to keep everything secret, you probably don't have a strategy. You probably have an illegal tax scheme.

Step Two: Implement Your Strategy Now

Once you have developed your offshore investment, business or moving strategy with your trusted advisors, implement.

There are two things people do wrong when they have a strategy like this. They either jump without getting the right advice from qualified advisors or, they wait too long. This is an area of tax law that is changing rapidly. If you wait too long to implement a plan, it may be out of date and you'll need to start over. Plus, if you start incorrectly, or just by default, you may end up having to do a costly fix to take advantage of the tax changes.

Don't be afraid to pull the trigger. If you have top-notch advisors, you'll have a great plan.

Step Three: Know What You Need to Report

We've talked about reporting requirements in every section of this book. You don't need to memorize the requirements or do it yourself. The purpose of the review is to let you know that there are a lot of reporting requirements. If you have a tax preparer who doesn't file anything for your offshore accounts, ask them why. It could be they didn't get the information they needed from you or it could be they don't understand the rules.

If you don't file, you're the one with the penalties and possible criminal charges. It's important to know what you need to file and make sure your CPA is aware of what is going on, as well.

Step Four: Catch Up Missed Filings

If you find out you've missed filing some of the reports in the past, you need to get in front of this right now. There have been changes to the voluntary disclosure program to make it much easier to come forward. But, if the IRS catches you first, all of your options go away.

Printed in Great Britain
by Amazon